Garden Flowers

Joan Compton

illustrated by Gwen Green

Hamlyn
London · New York · Sydney · Toronto

FOREWORD

This book is intended as a guide to those who wish to take up gardening as a hobby. Perhaps they wish to make a garden or to remake or alter an existing one of moderate size, involving the minimum of expense. Whatever the reason for this choice a garden can give the owners considerable pleasure and enjoyment.

The construction of a new garden is an impossible task to achieve in a few weeks, but, by the use of quick growing plants such as annuals, a good colourful show can be made the first year, and with herbaceous plants, rose trees and shrubs already going into the ground one can feel that a start has been made. Kindly neighbours will often give some small roots from their own garden which is a great help, and should never be refused. It is quite possible that the gardener may not care for the plant offered but this is not the moment to be choosy. These generous offerings may result in great similarity between local gardens, but this can be sorted out in a year or two.

It is hoped, therefore, that, by offering some suggestions regarding choice of plants, shrubs and decorative trees, immediate interest can be aroused and maintained throughout the first and possibly rather dull stages that must unfortunately precede the making of a new garden.

J.C.

The months and seasons mentioned in this book apply to temperate regions of the northern hemisphere – Europe, Canada and the northern United States.

Published by The Hamlyn Publishing Group Limited
London · New York · Sydney · Toronto
Astronaut House, Feltham, Middlesex, England

Copyright © The Hamlyn Publishing Group Limited 1969
Fourth impression 1975
ISBN 0 600 00087 7

Phototypeset by Oliver Burridge Filmsetting Limited, Crawley, Sussex
Colour separations by Schwitter Limited, Zurich
Printed in Spain by Mateu Cromo, Madrid

CONTENTS

INTRODUCTION

Making a garden

Unfortunately, the planning and preparation of a brand new garden does take time and may seem a very wearisome task. Patience and imagination are absolutely essential and, although after some weeks of rather dreary work one suddenly begins to see a lovely picture forming in the mind's eye, in the eyes of friends it may still be an expanse of mud. Planning the positions of beds, paths, trees, borders, steps, hedges and fences will probably remain a dream for some time but the day will come when one's patient efforts will at last begin to bring results. From that moment gardening will become enjoyable. There will be more setbacks of course, but there will be triumphs as well.

If remaking or replanning a garden is the object, it is best to avail oneself of as much as possible of what is in it already. Depending on the time of year one takes possession, it is unlikely that one will have much idea of what plants, or bulbs will make their appearance during the ensuing months. An existing garden is always more interesting to begin with because there are some established plants, even if not to one's own choice. The wish to change them or their positions is not really urgent and, although possibly there are lawns, hedges or walls to be adapted, in a brand new garden every single yard of ground has to be started from scratch, often on poor soil.

Too rapid elimination of existing plants proves a mistake. It is so easy to dig up and throw away firmly established plants only to regret their disappearance later. Existing plants give help in showing soil preference and, although a plant may not be just the colour one would choose, if it likes the soil in which it is growing, it is more sensible to choose a different colour in a similar plant than to replace it with something that does not like its surroundings and will never grow well in that particular district. In most areas certain plants do much better than others and it is very useful to be able to make a note of those that do well in a particular locality.

(*Top left*) Columbine (*Aquilegia*) and (*below*) *Delphinium*, variety 'Lamartine' (*left*) and *Liatris*

SOIL CULTIVATION

Character of the soil

One of the first jobs, in either a new or second-hand garden, is to discover something about the character of the soil. This can be done by digging down to a depth of at least two feet to get a rough idea of the different soil types.

Chalk soil, for instance, has a white chalk (lime) subsoil. It is a light soil that drains away easily and, because of this, it is necessary to dig in plenty of compost with generous applications of fertilizers. Iron and other associated minerals should be used once or twice a year.

Clay soils are cold and heavy and of little use for early crops. They are, however, suitable for plants such as roses and added organic matter will improve the texture and aeration. Drainage may also be necessary. Loam is an easily worked soil, and is often found in older gardens that have been cultivated for years. In this medium most plants grow well, especially if light applications of balanced fertilizers are given occasionally.

Peat soil is spongy and dark, in which heathers, azaleas and rhododendrons grow well but liming is necessary for many plants. Sandy soil is gritty, warm, and dries fast unless plenty of well rotted manure is added to retain moisture. Stony soil is also well drained and some added humus will help to hold in the moisture. Only the largest stones need removing. The removal of every stone will allow all of the soil particles to compact together and prevent air entering the soil.

To discover the nature of any soil, several samples should be collected from the garden, totalling about 1 lb. in weight, and mixed together. This should be allowed to dry in an airy place, and then sent to the nearest County Horticultural Officer or one of the bigger fertilizer companies for analysis to be made, with advice for remedying deficiencies.

Autumn or winter is the best time of year to carry out basic soil treatment. At least a month should be allowed to elapse after work is finished before any planting is started. In a previously cultivated garden, breaking up the ground so that the air can get in, adding farmyard manure, compost, and leaf-mould will feed the soil and help to give the roots and plants a better start during the new year.

If the garden soil is heavy in texture, such as a clay soil, then drainage may be necessary. Each trench should be dug to a depth of about 16 inches and lead to a ditch or soak-away. The bottom of the trench must be covered with gravel to a depth of about 6 inches and then re-topped with soil.

Clearing rough ground

During the clearance of uncultivated ground, the turf and weeds should first be stripped off with a spade. The turves should be stacked in a heap, grass sides downwards, where they can be left to rot down for compost, and any weeds with deep roots or underground creeping stems must be dug out and burned. When the ground is heavy, such as with clay soils, some simple drainage may be necessary. If this is so, trenches should be dug about 16 inches deep and 12 feet apart with a fall of about one inch in twenty, each trench leading to a ditch or soak-away. The bottom of each trench is then covered with gravel, followed with large stones or broken clinker to a depth of six inches and re-topped with the soil.

Double digging is essential for uncultivated soil, but soil already in good condition can be kept fertile for several years by single digging. A large heavy spade is not suitable for either single or double digging and a smaller, lighter spade generally proves more efficient as it is less tiring and quicker to use.

During double digging, a 10 inch wide trench the depth of the spade blade (one spit deep) must be dug across the end of the piece of ground and this excavated soil taken to the other end of the plot. A strip of earth, about six inches wide and one spit deep should be turned upside down and thrown to the back of the trench. It is not necessary to break up these clods of earth as frost will do this during the winter. If this procedure is continued clod by clod, row by row working backwards

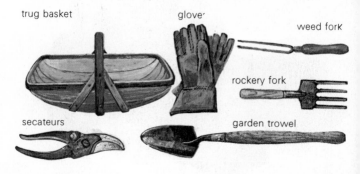

trug basket

glove

weed fork

rockery fork

secateurs

garden trowel

across the plot until the far end is reached, the final trench can be filled in with the soil barrowed from the first trench. The surface of the plot can be covered, before digging, with well-rotted compost or farmyard manure, which is then turned into the soil with each spadeful. Keeping the blade of the spade clean will help to make digging easy. Scraping all weeds into the trench will ensure that they are buried deeply.

(A) rake (B) edge-clipping shears (C) rubbish container (D) spade (E) wheelbarrow (F) shears (G) hoe (H) fork (I) garden hose

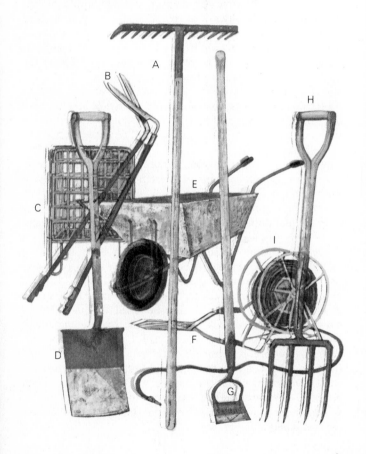

Ridging, raking and hoeing

One treatment is not sufficiently thorough for ground that is being cultivated for the first time and it is better to give the soil one more break-up. After that nature can do some work, during the winter, until, in the spring, seed sowing preparations begin and garden work becomes more interesting and brings the garden alive.

Ridging, which is the next breaking-up procedure, is simple although rather dull. A garden line, which is a short sturdy stake tied by a length of strong garden twine to another similar stake of the same height, must be driven firmly into the ground at opposite sides of the plot to be dug so that the cord between makes a taut guiding line for the spade. A trench about one foot wide should be dug along it, putting a spadeful of soil on one side of the trench, the next spadeful on the other side of the trench, and so on across the plot. The line and stakes must then be moved about two feet behind the first trench and the process continued until the whole plot has been dug. In this manner a large area of soil is left exposed to the weather and the large lumps of soil will be easier to hoe and rake in the spring, when, about a couple of weeks before sowing or planting, the ground is prepared for this purpose. Before raking, any large lumps of earth must be broken down with a fork and, if the soil is crumbly, as it should be after the effects of the winter weather, it will be quite easy to use a hoe over the plot until the soil is fine enough to be raked level and a fine tilth produced.

For seed sowing the soil must be broken down to a really fine tilth. This should be done when the ground is fairly dry, by walking to and fro over the area in which seeds are to be sown and pulling a rake over the surface to remove any large stones or hard lumps. The soil must then be raked once more before sowing. If the garden is being re-made the elimination of weeds should be given very careful attention. Thistles, Creeping Buttercup, Ground Elder and Bindweed roots should be removed by digging the beds and borders in early spring, carefully picking out every scrap of root and burning them. After this the use of the hoe between plants whenever possible will keep the soil open, destroy weeds, help to control certain pests and aerate the ground.

A compost heap is used to convert most of the garden rubbish into an excellent soil conditioner. A wire framework will help to keep the heap tidy.

Compost

Compost is invaluable, for once started it will go on for years, yielding an extremely useful return for the few feet of space it occupies, converting most of the garden rubbish into an excellent soil conditioner. The compost heap should be sited in a readily accessible corner of the garden without being too prominently displayed. A shrub or hedge will often help to disguise this feature, and a frame-work of wire netting with one side easily removable, will keep the heap tidy. Grass cuttings, dead leaves and flowers, vegetable waste and any soft-wooded hedge cuttings can be put on it, but not weeds or any hard-stemmed rubbish, which are better burned. Every nine or ten inches a layer of soil should be put over the rubbish and the heap turned over with a fork about every three weeks, watering through a fine rose if the weather is dry to keep the compost damp. When the heap is about three feet high it can be moved out of its framework and a new heap started. The compost is ready for use when it is brown and has a manure-like appearance. It is useful for lightening heavy soil, holding moisture in light soil, and as a plant food for all soils.

Sterilized soil is useful for seed growing and pricking out, since this process destroys all diseases and pests. All that is necessary is to sieve some good garden soil and soak it thoroughly in an appropriate dilution of formaldehyde. This is usually $\frac{1}{2}$ pint in 3 gallons of water, although there are several proprietary brands on the market with their own directions for use. The soil must be turned continuously as it is treated, then stored away from untreated soil. It should not be used for 4 to 6 weeks but turned periodically to disperse fumes. A useful seed compost can be made from two parts of sterilized soil, one part good peat and one part coarse garden sand. To each bushel of this mixture is added $\frac{3}{4}$ ounce of ground chalk or limestone and $\frac{1}{2}$ ounce of superphosphate. Many seedsmen offer sterilized seed compost for sale, ready for use. John Innes seed compost is excellent for starting off seeds, while potting compost is used when potting plants.

Many different types of garden can be designed and the three plans on the following page indicate three distinct types of lay-out that can be adapted as the gardener desires.

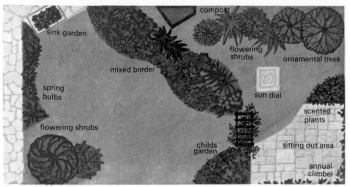

PLAN A

- compost
- sink garden
- flowering shrubs
- mixed border
- ornamental trees
- spring bulbs
- sun dial
- scented plants
- flowering shrubs
- sitting out area
- childs garden
- annual climber

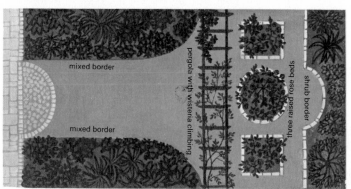

PLAN B

- mixed border
- mixed border
- pergola with wisteria climbing
- three raised rose beds
- shrub border

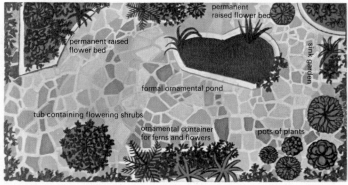

PLAN C

- permanent raised flower bed
- permanent raised flower bed
- sink garden
- formal ornamental pond
- tub containing flowering shrubs
- ornamental container for ferns and flowers
- pots of plants

PLANNING A FLOWER GARDEN

Lay-out plans

Once garden preparations have been started by digging, draining, and clearing, it is time to start planning some of the first details of a new garden, leaving, as previously suggested, an existing garden to yield up its secrets gradually during the spring and summer months. The first thing to decide about planning a new garden is the amount of ground one wishes to cultivate, and whether there are any particular features to be embodied. If, for instance, a rock-garden or a sheltered sunny corner for outdoor meals is wanted, these more permanent features are better planned first.

In the lay-out plan *A* a garden on one level is pictured, giving space for a mixed border including flowering shrubs, some flowering trees and an archway dividing the lawn, supporting climbers. It terminates in a brick-paved corner surrounded on two sides by beds of sweetly-scented annuals and backed by a fence against which annual climbers are planted to provide quick coverage for the first summer, while perennials are making a permanent home for themselves

Border based on Plan B

between the annuals. Tucked away is a compost heap, a child's garden, and a sink garden for miniature rock plants.

In the next plan *B* a broad central path is bordered on each side by wide beds filled with spring bulbs, biennials and annuals. This leads to a pergola running at right angles to the path and borders, behind which are raised rose beds. A shrub border forms a boundary at the end of the garden. Plan *C* is for a modern type of small courtyard garden paved with stone, a small, formal pool providing a point of interest. Climbing plants are growing against the house walls from small beds in the paving and a variety of stone and earthenware urns, pots and bowls contain fuchsias, geraniums, lilies and camellias. Evergreen shrubs are decorative, while low troughs contain brightly coloured annuals.

The initial cost of this last type of garden is higher than the cost of cultivating a strip of bare earth but a courtyard is quicker to construct and saves a great deal of labour. It is inexpensive to maintain, and provides the equivalent of another room for six months of the year, blending well with newly built houses. Even the rubble left behind by builders can be used in the foundations for the paving and pool.

Some of the types of plant containers described in Plan C

Coreopsis

Foxglove

Canterbury Bell

16

Annuals and biennials

It would be quite easy to extend a formal garden, such as the one previously mentioned, by making a lawn, with perhaps some small flowering trees growing in the grass, which leads to a very informal 'wild' garden, where nursery beds could be made for growing the annuals and biennials that will be needed for filling the troughs and urns in the courtyard as they are required. Flowers for cutting could also be grown here together with some informal foliage, herbaceous plants and roses. If this area could be raised above the lawn level, a stone supporting wall, uncemented, would achieve the dual purpose of holding the soil in place, and providing a home, in the crevices between the stones, for a number of rock plants, especially for those which have a trailing habit.

Whatever may be decided about the planning of the new garden, many of the first plants will be grown from seed. An annual is a plant that is sown where it is to grow, blooms and dies in the same year. A half-hardy annual is sown a few weeks earlier under glass in a cold greenhouse or frame and the tiny seedlings are pricked out, then planted into their flowering positions when all danger of frost is over. Biennials are sown one year and come into flower the following year. Good examples of some of the commonest grown in England are Canterbury Bells, Sweet Williams, Foxgloves, Wallflowers and Forget-me-nots.

Annuals are excellent for brightening dull corners, especially while the garden is being re-planned.

Hardy annuals require a medium, well-drained soil, light and air. They do not like dense shade, or growing under trees, and the thorough, deep cultivation of the soil in autumn, as previously discussed, is of great importance. Annuals flower best in not too rich a soil, where they might tend to go to leaf rather than flower, but if the soil is very light it must be firmed well before sowing. Firming is done by treading or rolling the surface of the soil to make certain there are no hollows underneath, then on germination the young roots come into direct contact with the tiny particles of soil from which they are fed. The soil should not be worked when wet and sticky for this might cause tight packing and seal off the air and lack of ventilation can actually kill off the young seedlings.

Virginia Stock

Linum

Anemone

Although there are a few exceptions, the best soil for growing most annuals and biennials is a medium loam. This will not be too rich but will contain sufficient plant food. It should also contain enough sand or grit to enable the soil to be raked to provide a good seed bed.

It is usually best to select a site in full sunlight for sowing annuals, but some, such as godetia and pansies, can be grown in partial shade. Usually the effect of growing these plants in the shade, however, is to increase the height of the plants and give them weak stems. Flower production is also delayed. If much of the garden is partially shaded part of the problem can be solved by sowing annuals under glass earlier than they would be sown outside.

Whatever the type of soil, it should be well dug to give good drainage. If the existing soil is very dry, rotted manure can be added and if it is a sticky soil, coarse grit and strawy manure.

Bonemeal can be added to encourage not only plant growth but also flower production.

To get the best results when sowing the soil must be friable, moist and warm. It is far better to delay for a while than to risk sowing seed in soil that is still cold, but it is impossible to give a date for seed sowing since weather conditions can be so variable – it is possible to tell, by feeling the soil, when there is warmth in it, and the end of April is usually about the time. The method of sowing annuals in drills is probably the best, because it enables easy thinning and weeding. The use of a hoe will keep the soil open between the rows, which need not be in straight lines, particularly for a border and could be vertical, horizontal, diagonal or curved. Each patch of drills could well be a different shape and the final result will look all the better at flowering time – for the different flowers will merge into one colourful carpet. The seeds should not be buried too deeply and very small seed should barely be covered. A good guide to follow is to sow at a depth of twice the diameter of the seed, varying the depth proportionately with the size of the seed. It must be remembered that the garden line should be removed before sowing and covering the seeds.

Drills should be drawn with the corner of a hoe (*left*), the seed sown along the drill and lightly raked in (*right*).

The thinning process should be gradual but no seedling should be left in a crowded position. Distance is determined by growth habit.

Seeds can also be scattered over a chosen area, or sown broadcast as this process is termed. Seed sown this way should be scattered thinly and lightly raked in. The soil should be pressed down firmly with the back of a spade so that one can be certain that the seeds are in contact with the soil. When this is omitted unequal germination of the seed sometimes occurs, some seeds remaining dry for quite long periods.

Large seeds, such as those of nasturtiums, are better pushed into the soil, to a depth of about half an inch. These can, of course, be better spaced at sowing time.

If the seeds are sown in drills, the drills should be drawn with the corner of a hoe or the back of a rake. Each group of seeds should be marked as soon as they are sown with a clearly written garden lable marking the position and also the name. If indelible ink is used on the label it will remain for as long as is necessary.

Pea sticks, laid across the drills, will discourage birds from eating the newly-sown seed. These should be removed when the seedlings have appeared and can be broken down into sticks of a suitable size to support them as they grow.

If the drills are thoroughly watered before the seed is sown, the soil will most probably retain sufficient moisture until after germination. A watering can with a very fine rose should be used to prevent the soil becoming firmly packed down. After the seeds have germinated the plants should be watered mainly in the mornings, so that any surplus moisture has time to drain off before the evening. On no account, however, should the seedlings be allowed to become too dry.

The plants must be thinned immediately they are large enough to handle to enable the best possible development. The first thinning can be done when a pair of ordinary leaves have been formed, that is, leaves typical of the plant and not the seed leaves which are often different from the usual leaves.

The thinning process should be gradual but in no instance should a seedling be left that will crowd its neighbour. This probably means that at the first thinning the seedlings should be spaced one to two inches apart. A second thinning should be done a week or ten days later, according to the rate of growth, and a final thinning should space the plants sufficiently far apart to allow them to develop fully without crowding.

Distance between the seedlings can be determined by their habit of growth and expected height as given on the outside of the seed packet. More often than not, however, the correct distance for spacing the final plants is also given on the packet as well.

It is very important that each plant has sufficient room to develop freely. For example, a bushy, branching type of annual such as a *Calendula*, the Pot Marigold, will need a space of 6 to 9 inches from its neighbours on all sides, while a more slender-stemmed annual, such as *Viscaria*, will require only about half that space, preferring some support from the nearby plants.

Normally all annuals are raised from seed in the manner already described but some annuals can also be increased by taking cuttings, thus preserving for at least another year a plant with perhaps unusual colouring. This method does have disadvantages, however, and seed raising is always preferable because it produces stronger plants.

It is quite possible to propagate annuals and biennials from their own seeds. All these plants produce a lot of seeds and these can be collected, when ripe, and thoroughly dried before storing for use the following spring. One disadvantage of home saved seed is that the pollen that fertilized the flower may have come from a wild strain and the gardener should be prepared for a proportion of inferior plants.

Half-hardy annuals and biennials

Half-hardy annuals are sown in boxes, for they need a longer growing season than annuals and will not stand even the slightest degree of frost in the seedling stage. The principles of sowing half-hardy annuals are similar to those for annuals, but the first part of a half-hardy annual's life must be spent in a frame or greenhouse from which all frost can be excluded. It is probably wiser for the beginner to gardening to buy ready-made sterilized seed compost for the first efforts at growing these plants. The containers used will probably be the usual standard size wooden or plastic seed boxes, nine inches wide, fourteen inches long and two to three inches deep. These are easily arranged on shelves or benches, and, provided they are always thoroughly washed with soapy water and well dried between use, they can be used over and over again.

The bottom of the box should be covered with a layer of broken pots to ensure good drainage, followed by a layer of rough peat about $\frac{3}{4}$ inch deep, and finally filled up with seed compost to within $\frac{1}{2}$ inch of the top of the box. This must be pressed down firmly and evenly. The compost will probably be made firm more easily by using a flat oblong piece of wood roughly a third the size of the box, which has had a simple handle fixed to the top for ease of use. The compost will have just the right firmness if pressed down with the fingers and then the flat board. Some hours before seed sowing the compost must be thoroughly dampened and this should provide sufficient moisture to ensure germination of most small seeds. The seeds should be sowed evenly and thinly and, if they are very small, simply placed thinly on the surface of the compost and pressed into the compost with the wooden presser. Larger seeds should be lightly covered to about twice their depth by sifting compost through a fine sieve directly on to the top of the seeds. The boxes can be covered with a piece of glass to ensure a moist atmosphere but the glass must be turned over each day to prevent too much condensation forming on the underside. A piece of newspaper placed over the top of the glass will protect the seeds from the drying rays of the sun. If the weather becomes excessively hot it sometimes can be better to paint whitewash over the greenhouse roof and thus make temperatures generally lower.

Larkspur (*right*) with Scabious
(*centre*) and *Phlox* (*bottom*)

23

Immediately the seedlings begin to appear, the covering paper and glass should both be removed so that air can be obtained by the plants. Once the seeds have germinated growth will be rapid. The seedlings will probably soon fill the seed box and each seedling will then be competing for air, light, and moisture. Thus, before they become too crowded, each seedling must be transferred individually to other boxes to give them room to develop. This process is known as pricking out.

The plants should not be allowed to become overcrowded before they are pricked out. The same procedure and similar boxes should be used as were prepared for sowing the seed, but the seed compost is replaced by potting compost, which has more feeding qualities for the fast growing seedlings, which should not be deprived of nutrients.

crocking the seed box

filling with compost

levelling off

watering

The usual number of little plants to a box is about four dozen, spaced $\frac{1}{2}$ inch apart either way. To ensure equal spacing the positions can be marked out on the soil with a dibber, which is a piece of pointed wood about the diameter of a thick pencil four inches in length. The planting holes must be sufficiently deep and wide to take the roots comfortably, then each seedling must be carefully removed and held by the lower leaves, not the stem, and placed so that the roots just touch the bottom of the hole. Gently turning the soil with the dibber to leave the lowest leaves just above the level of the compost, care must be taken not to bury the crown. The seedlings can be watered finely to settle them, the contents of each box labelled and placed in a light, airy position out of draughts with the new seedlings shaded with tissue paper to avoid their leaves becoming scorched by sun.

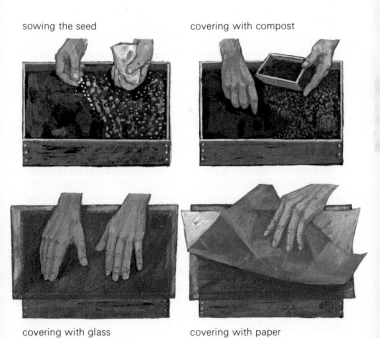

sowing the seed

covering with compost

covering with glass

covering with paper

The hardening-off process follows pricking out, in order to acclimatize the seedlings to open-air conditions before planting out. The boxes should gradually be given more time in the open air each day, in a sheltered position, and all put back into a frame or greenhouse before evening until they are sturdy enough to plant out in border or beds; it is important to keep them moist during the hardening-off period.

The instructions that are given on the seed packets generally include the best time to plant out. Sometimes seeds sown under glass are in fact hardy plants, sown in this manner to protect them from insect pests. These plants can go into the garden in about April, although it is wise to choose a period of mild weather to give the plants a good start.

Half-hardy plants should not be put out in the open until all danger of frost is over, and this, of course, will vary with the locality. No plant that has been grown in a greenhouse or under glass should be planted out without previous hardening, whether the plants are hardy varieties or not.

A trowel should be used for planting out and a hole should be made deep enough to take the roots without causing them to be bent. The soil around the plants should be as firm as possible to prevent the roots becoming dry. Each plant should be given enough room to develop to its full size and no thinning out is done among plants set out from seed boxes or pots.

Biennials should be sown in early summer in nursery beds when all danger of frost is over. It is best to locate the nursery bed in a sheltered position using well-cultivated soil, raked down to a fine tilth. They are best if sown in shallow drills, with a garden line as a guide, and then pricked out, preferably in showery weather when the seedlings are 2 to 3 inches high, into rows 12 inches apart with 6 to 8 inches between plants. They can be planted into flowering positions in the autumn and they will flower the following summer.

Most annuals and biennials not only make attractive garden flowers, but also can be cut for house decorations. Most of these plants will not travel well and should be put into water immediately they are cut. Never allow the water in the vase or container to fall below the base of the highest stem. If this does happen, an air-lock in the stem will prevent water being absorbed by the flowers.

Lupins (*right*) and
Chrysanthemum carinatum
(*bottom left*). Wallflowers
(*bottom right*)

27

SHRUBS

Selection of garden shrubs

Shrubs, variegated, flowering and evergreen, have become very popular during the last few years. Once established they demand a minimum of attention and a shrub border will be interesting all the year round, even in the winter and early spring. One thing is very important and that is that they must be given enough space in which to grow. It is easy to plant young shrubs far too close together which will mean, in two or three years, that they will be so overcrowded that much of their charm will be lost. It is far better to fill in gaps with annuals each year and since they are shallow-rooted they will not interfere with the growth of the shrubs, but will give colour and gaiety to the scene until the shrubs can provide this for themselves. If there is a good nursery in one's own district it is better to purchase locally because the nurseryman will be able to advise on the choice of subjects. The shrubs described in the following pages are not difficult to grow and should do well in most districts. Generally speaking it is wiser not to pamper shrubs with a rich diet or too much shelter for the result could be lush, sappy growth that would not stand a hard winter. Poorish soil in a slightly more exposed position will produce a tougher growth.

Elaeagnus pungens aurea is a very colourful evergreen shrub

Shrubs have been increasing in popularity as a garden plant during recent years because once they are established they will require a minimum of attention. The choice is basically dependant on the wishes of the gardener, the type of soil and the amount of space that is available.

HEDERA COLCHICA DENTATA VARIEGATA JASMINUM NUDIFLORUM

CORNUS
ALBA SPAETHII

RHODODENDRON
LADY
CHAMBERLAIN

ROSMARINUS
OFFICINALIS

MAHONIA
AQUIFOLIUM

ERICA MEDITERRANEA

ERICA VAGANS

SKIMMIA
JAPONICA

BERGENIA

HELLEBORUS ORIENTALIS

with green and bright yellow foliage providing a cheerful patch of colour during winter and spring. A slow grower, it eventually reaches a height of 5 to 6 feet but tends to spread liking an open, sheltered, dryish border, or a position against south or west walls. It should be planted in April or September.

Garrya elliptica is another hardy evergreen shrub about 7 feet in height, which bears 12 inch long grey-green catkins from November to the end of February. It has dark green rather leathery-looking leaves and likes ordinary well-drained soil in an open situation or against south or west walls. *Mahonia japonica* starts to flower at the beginning of December, giving long racemes of scented, pale yellow flowers and glossy green, pinnate leaves that turn red and orange in the autumn. It likes a peaty soil but succeeds in open ground in a limy clay soil if it has adequate drainage. Although it will grow to a height of 5 feet, it has better leaf growth if kept to a lower height by cutting off the flowering heads once they have flowered. It is a very sturdy plant, and will withstand exposed and extremely cold conditions.

Shrubs used in the border

Garrya elliptica

Chimonanthus praecox is a hardy, deciduous flowering shrub which has yellow and red flowers blooming in December, that eventually reaches a height of 6 feet. The scent of this shrub is quite delicious and a small spray of it kept in water will perfume a whole room. Passing the shrub as it grows against a wall on a sunny winter's day will also make this lovely scent noticeable. It likes a deep rich soil in a position against south or west walls or fences. In February all the shoots that have flowered should be cut away to within one inch of their base, except those required to furnish the plant with branches.

Corylopsis pauciflora grows to a height of 4 feet. The clusters of primrose-yellow, scented flowers in February are borne on the bare branches and the leaves that follow the flowers provide attractive small-leaved foliage of green edged with light brown, *Corylopsis spicata* is a slightly taller shrub with hanging bunches of pale primrose-yellow cowslip-scented flowers on leafless branches. *C. spicata* is slightly more hardy than *C. pauciflora*. Neither need pruning for several years and then only lightly, to keep the shrubs free of dead wood. *Kerria japonica floriplena* has a height of 6 to 9 feet with double yellow flowers in April and May. This is a deciduous shrub, but the bare green stems fan out from ground level providing interest in the border in winter. It likes a position in good ordinary soil, preferably against a west or north wall, or a hedge, to protect it from the wind, which is apt to mark its flowers. Pruning can be done in May or June after flowering by cutting off old and weak shoots only.

The forsythia family are lovely at the beginning of March and are hardy, deciduous shrubs that like ordinary soil, a sunny sheltered position in the shrubbery, or can be grown as a hedge, or even trained as a climber against south and west walls. The rich yellow-flowered *Forsythia spectabilis* is one of the best, with large flowers in profusion, followed by foliage that turns to rich autumnal colours in September. If cut while still in bud, brought into the house in February, and kept in a jug or bucket of deep water in a moderate temperature, the flowers will gradually open out about a month before they flower in the garden. It is a very popular plant with flower arrangers, especially for church decoration, and if the branches are cut for the house, this is usually quite sufficient pruning.

Daphne laureola is an evergreen shrub with small pale green scented flowers that appear in February and March. *Daphne mezereum* is free-flowering and easy to grow with either scented purple or white flowers (alba) in March, followed by pale green berries and leaves. It grows to a height of 3 to 5 feet but, unfortunately, has a life of only about seven years and needs no pruning, appreciating a sunny, sheltered position. The Dogwoods *(Cornus)* are grown both for their deciduous foliage and for their coloured stems, which in winter are most decorative. *Cornus alba spaethii* has yellow-edged leaves during the summer, with crimson stems, during the winter. *C. alba elegantissima* has coral coloured stems in winter, and silvery variegated leaves in summer. *C. alba westonbirt* has very bright red stems and green leaves. They all grow to a height of 8 feet and need no pruning, although the colour of the stem is improved if they are cut back hard in the spring. They prefer an ordinary soil together with plenty of moisture.

Skimmia japonica

Skimmias are hardy evergreen shrubs, berry-bearing with ornamental foliage and flowers that are fragrant but inconspicuous. Some species, notably *Skimmia japonica*, produce male and female flowers on separate plants. They like ordinary soil that is not shallow or dry, also part shade of full sun. They survive an exposed position. *S. foremanii* has white hermaphrodite flowers in spring followed by red berries in late summer, while *S. rubella* has pink fragrant male flowers in April. *Fatsia japonica* is an evergreen, slightly tender, shrub with large, handsome leaves. It likes a sheltered position and a little protection in very severe winter weather, especially from gales. It sometimes grows to a height of 12 feet with long side branches and its huge leaves grow in crowns at the top of the branches. The ivory flower stems, with their clusters of tiny cream flowers, appear at the apex of each crown.

Viburnums are an interesting group of shrubs and most are scented. *Viburnum carlesii* with clusters of pale pink buds, opening to white in April and May, is very sweetly scented; so too is *V. fragrans* with clusters of pale pink flowers in winter. *V. opulus sterile*, the Snowball Tree or Guelder Rose, is fairly tall, attaining a height of 10 to 12 feet, with ball-shaped flower heads that start pale green in June turning gradually to white. The foliage is colourful in autumn, and scarlet berries add to its attractive appearance. Another, *V. tinus*, is a hardy evergreen, with pink buds opening to white, which flowers from autumn to April. It is a quick growing shrub that makes a rounded bush about 10 feet in diameter. It is ideal for softening the corners of a building or concealing ugly places, as well as giving welcome sprays of foliage in winter. *V.* 'Eve Price' has deep rosy-red buds, and later, in favourable weather, berries of metallic blue. *Choisya ternata* or Mexican Orange is a hardy evergreen, with glossy green leaves. It has clusters of scented, single, white flowers which resemble orange blossom in May, and again in autumn. It likes an ordinary soil with the addition of a little peat or leaf-mould, in a sunny sheltered position, and grows well in chalky soils in maritime positions.

The Weigelias are deciduous shrubs that flourish in any good garden soil with an occasional mulching to conserve moisture, for they enjoy moist root conditions. They like slight shade, and should be pruned directly after flowering by shortening the shoots that have borne the flowers. The colours obtainable are pink, crimson, white, and yellow and they flower in May and June, growing to a height of approximately 5 feet with graceful arching branches. The yellow *Weigelia middenorffiana* is particularly unusual, while *W. praecox*, which is rose coloured, is the earliest to flower.

Weigela praecox variegata

Ribes sanguineum

Pyracantha crenato-serrata likes an ordinary well-drained soil in full sun. It can be trained as a hedge or against a fence or wall and is evergreen, with small white flowers in June, followed by clusters of coral berries. It should be pruned or trimmed where necessary in March. *Ribes sanguineum*, the Flowering Currant which has rose-coloured panicles of flowers in May before the leaves, is a hardy deciduous shrub and needs little attention if given a sunny position. Some of the older wood can be removed after flowering. Although some people object to the smell of this shrub, this is barely perceptible out of doors and if cut when in bud and the branches put in deep water in the house, the flowers will gradually come into blossom, rather paler than when flowering out of doors. It looks very attractive, and the smell is not apparent when 'forced' in this way. There is a white-flowered variety *R. album* and a fine deep red *R. splendens*. The foliage of all varieties colours well on the bush in autumn.

Pernettya micronata and its varieties *P. atrococcinea* and *P. lilacina*, are also evergreen with small insignificant white flowers in spring, followed by pink and mauve berries in summer that last until the following spring. It can be grown with good effect on a rockery but some control over roots is advisable as it is rather an invasive shrub. *Pernettya* grows to a height of 2 feet, and is better grown in front of the border where the sun can ripen the berries. *P. pumila* has pink or white berries and is more suitable for the rockery as it is smaller.

Cytisus 'Broom' is a deciduous hardy shrub and the different varieties provide wonderful flower colourings in May. They are not difficult to grow, enjoying hungry stony soils and dry positions and should be pruned after flowering, by shortening the old shoots to the base of promising young ones, avoiding cutting into the old wood. *C. albus* or White Spanish Broom has a height of 10 feet, with gold, scented flowers and foliage and shoots covered with fine silky hairs. *C. praecox* has creamy yellow flowers and grows to 4 to 6 feet. *C. burkwoodii* has red flowers growing to 4 to 5 feet while the flowers of

Elaeagnus

Chaenomeles

C. purpureus are purple and the shrub reaches a height of 1½ feet. All these shrubs are hardy varieties.

Ceanothus make very attractive wall shrubs. Both evergreen and deciduous varieties exist but the evergreen ones are not quite so hardy. The flowers are mainly blue and although there are some white varieties obtainable, the blue ones seem to be easier to grow and more effective in colouring. *C. caeruleus* also known as *C. azureus* gives blue flowers from July until autumn frost and is 8 to 10 feet in height. Old wood should be pruned fairly hard in March. These can all be grown as specimen shrubs, but are usually better for wall protection.

Fuchsias can be grown in an ordinary deep, fairly rich soil in borders, in a bed to themselves, or in tubs in a courtyard, and the colour combinations in the pendulous blooms are a constant source of delight. A draughty position should be avoided and in a sheltered, sunny position they will flower from June to September or until frost. Pinching out the points of the shoots frequently in the early summer will induce bushy growth and an occasional feed of liquid fertilizer is also extremely beneficial. All the shoots close to the base should be pruned off in early January and the roots protected with a cover of dry litter or leaves. *Fuchsia magellanica* has scarlet and purple flowers, *F. cornica* scarlet, *F. discolour* purple and red and *F. gracilis* scarlet and purple. The many other colours in both double and single flowers are endless.

Berberis are an extensive family of easily grown shrubs, some evergreen, some deciduous, the former grown for the beauty of their flowers and the latter for autumn colouring and berries. Many make good hedges and there are over 170 species known to cultivation, of which most are ornamental.

Choisya ternata

They can be grown from seed sown one inch deep in a sheltered border in November and the resultant plants will show considerable and interesting variations. Plants will grow anywhere except in dense shade but they prefer warm, sunny positions and thrive on dry, sandy or chalky soil. Deciduous species are better for an occasional thinning out of older, darker coloured wood in winter but evergreen species do not require pruning. Some of the most decorative of the deciduous varieties cultivated are; *B. aggreta*, height 6 feet with coral berries; *B. chillanensis*, height 6 feet with yellow and orange flowers followed by black berries; *B. polantha*, 6 feet with large clusters of salmon-red berries and *B. thunbergii*, also 6 feet high, with brilliant autumn foliage and red berries. Evergreen species include *B. darwinii*, which has dense growth suitable for hedging, with orange flowers in April to May, followed by plum coloured berries and *B. julianae* that also has dense growth, making a good 8 foot high screen, with dark blue berries. *B. lologensis* has gold flowers, suffused with apricot, and is a very handsome shrub that grows to a height of 8 feet.

Berberis darwinii in flower (*above*) and fruit (*below*)

ANNUAL BORDERS

Planning the border

Once the shrub border has been planned, planted and labelled, it is a good time to make plans for an annual border within the shrub border, to provide plenty of colour for the first year while the shrubs are settling down, and making their first season's growth. It must be remembered, however, that development will be slow in the initial stages. Whether one grows all one's own annuals from seed, or takes a short cut by purchasing at least some seedlings, depends on the individual but in either case one should aim at making bold groups and drifts of annuals that will look much more effective.

This effect can easily be produced if seed is sown where it is to flower, but if some of the seedlings are bought the same must be done when they are planted into the border. A few scattered seedlings will be lost in an ordinary border but a whole boxful planted in one mass will be much more telling and half, or even a quarter of a boxful, planted in a group,

The annual border

LARKSPUR	LUPIN		LARKSPUR
CALENDULA	HELIANTHUS		GODETIA
ASTER	SHIRLEY POPPY	MALOPE	NIGELLA

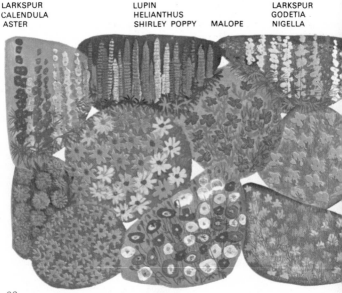

allowing, of course, the necessary space between each seedling when planted, will make much more of an impact.

If seedlings are bought, it is important to make quite certain that they have been hardened off by the nursery before they were bought and they should not be planted in the border before the beginning of May, or until all danger of frost is over. When the annual border is planned the tallest plants are usually planted at the back, or towards the centre of the border, if it is to be viewed on all sides, and the shortest at the front or edges. This plan should not be adhered to too rigidly, however, because a more haphazard arrangement of the different subjects, with the heights of the plants at different levels, makes the border look natural and informal.

Colour arranging, whether it is blending or contrasting, is a matter for individual taste and it is worth making notes of the colour combinations and plants that are found particularly pleasing for future reference. These notes on planting and border arrangement apply, of course, to any annual border, whether it is in conjunction with shrubs or for annuals alone.

STER
TOCKS
ALENDULA

LUPIN
CALIFORNIAN POPPY
LINUM

ALYSSUM

ASTER
CANDYTUFT
CHRYSANTHEMU

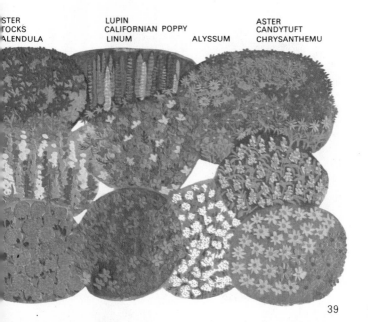

Alyssum

Amaranthus

Malope

Godetia

40

Easy-growing annuals

The following suggestions are for simple well-known easily grown annuals from which it should be possible to make a selection for the first year. Often these are obtainable in varying colours and heights, which makes it possible to get variation in different positions in the border without having to sow too many different varieties of seed. If the flowers of all annuals are removed as soon as they begin to fade, the flowering period will be extended, besides making the border look well tended. Some of the more interesting seed heads of the annuals can be kept for drying for many different types of winter flower arrangement, but these will be dealt with elsewhere in the book.

Annual Aster can be grown as an annual in the south, but is better sown under glass as a half-hardy annual, in more northerly districts. There is a large colour range obtainable, white, pale yellow, many shades of pink, red, mauves and purple and there are double and single varieties. Californian Giant Asters, with long stems, and large double flowers are very suitable for cutting, and reach a height of $2\frac{1}{2}$ feet. Ostrich Plume Asters, with large feathery heads of loosely twisted petals are 2 feet high. Rayonantha Asters are a new strain of large 2 foot tall double flowers with slender quilled petals, while Fire Devil is a very striking Aster with bright red flowers, that is 2 feet high and very good for cutting. Powder Puffs, which are double Asters in a mixture of many colours, are 2 feet in height.

Amaranthus (Love-Lies-Bleeding) is a useful species of annual which makes an unusual group among the more familiar patches of flowers. Growing to a height of 2 to 3 feet, it has pendulous, dark red racemes of tiny flowers that look rather long like tassels. There is also a pale green form, *A. viridis*, and both of these look very striking when growing and are much used for flower decoration. It is advisable to strip off their leaves after cutting, and they can be carefully dried for winter, as the colour of the spikes remains unchanged for some time. *Amaranthus* 'Molten Fire' has dark foliage and scarlet heads, and is a vigorous, bushy plant which is particularly striking in large groups, although it is not quite as tall ($1\frac{1}{2}$ feet) as the previous two forms.

Annual Chrysanthemum is a very hardy annual. The flowers last well in water and the average height is 2 feet, although there is a dwarf variety available, Monarch Court Jesters, at a height of one foot. There are both single and double varieties available, many in white or yellow. *Chrysanthemum carinatum burridgeannum* is about 2 feet high with white, single flowers that have a zone of yellow at the base of the petals and dark maroon coloured centres. *C. carinatum* 'Lord Beaconsfield' has bronze-red and bronze zones on varying ground colours and a height of 2 feet.

Atriplex is an easily raised annual, grown mainly for the colour of its leaves. The form *hortensis cupreata*, with red leaves on violet stems, and the yellow-foliaged variety are both attractive when sown in groups among the flowering annuals. Both reach a height of 4 feet and are useful for flower arrangement.

Alyssum is a good low-growing annual to sow in drifts in the front of a border, letting it make inroads between some of the taller plants. Most of the annual alyssum are sweetly scented, in shades of white, various shades of pink (Rosie Day is a new deep pink form) and deep and pale purple. Height is 4 to 6 inches.

Candytuft *(Iberis)* is, like Alyssum, a fairly low, easily grown annual, with more height variation around 8 to 9 inches. The colours range between white, rose, and purple.

Eschsholzia (Californian Poppy) is a showy annual about 12 inches high with glaucous foliage that likes sun, and good drainage. It is a perennial, better treated as a hardy annual in this country although it can be sown in autumn in a sunny position where winter frosts are not severe. *E. gloaming* has deep, coral-rose flowers and *E. mandain* flowers are deep orange shaded, crimson.

Godetia is a popular, very showy annual with a long flowering season, good for cutting. The azalea-flowered varieties of Godetia are particularly attractive, 15 to 18 inches high, in colours of bright pink, bright crimson and salmon, similar to the taller double Grandiflora, 2 feet high, in shades of white, shell pink, rich pink, cherry red and crimson. The tall doubles may be sown in place in the autumn in an open situation and will then produce plants 3 feet high the following year.

Morning Glory (*below*) an annual climber

(*Above*) the half-hardy annual, *Cobea scandens*

43

44

Larkspur is a very useful hardy annual which grows well from seed sown in spring where it is to flower, or can be sown in autumn, in August or September when longer spikes of flowers, up to 5 feet in height, will result the following summer. When the seed is germinating it is rather attractive to slugs so the use of slug pellets at this time is advisable. There is a choice of heights of the plant from $1\frac{1}{2}$ feet (dwarf) to 4 feet (regal) and, for a border, the mixed packets of seeds in which there are shades of white, mixed pinks, mauve, purple and blue, all blending well together, are ideal.

Linum (Flax) is a slender annual 12 to 18 inches high that is attractive in the border. The petals have a silky sheen and rustle in the breeze. There is a scarlet *Grandiflorum* 'Venice Red' and also a white, pink and blue form.

Lupins *(Lupinus)* are usually classed as a hardy perennial, but seeds of the annual lupins can also be obtained, which are just right for the annual border and flower for a long period, with a good colour range. *L. mutabilis* grows to about 3 to 4 feet, has scented flowers in a good range of colours.

Malope is a handsome annual that is fine in masses and which grows to 3 feet, seldom requiring staking. It flowers from June until September and likes an open situation in the garden, preferably in light soil.

Marigold *(Calendula)* is an accommodating annual. It is perfectly hardy, will grow in poor soil and can be sown in the autumn in the open, or in spring. It flowers from June until the autumn and both single and double varieties are available, in shades of yellow, orange, and apricot.

Nigella (Love-in-a-Mist) is a favourite annual growing to $1\frac{1}{2}$ feet, with green deeply-cut foliage, semi-double flowers, and most decorative seed pods that have persistent stigmas resembling horns, which are used with great effect, both fresh and dried, for flower decoration. The best known Nigella is *N. damascena*, which has varieties with bright blue, dark blue and pure white flowers. *N.* 'Persian Rose' is a new form that has flowers that open pink and deepen to rose colour, but for the annual border, the forms of *N. damascena* are especially recommended.

Canary Creeper (*far left*) and Nasturtium

Papaver (Poppies) look charming in groups in the border and there are many types from which to choose, although many of them are grown as perennials or biennials. Two which can be grown as annuals are the Shirley Poppies, both double and single, which are now obtainable in a wide range of colours, including white, all shades of pink, and salmon. The other very decorative poppy is the Opium Poppy, *Papaver somniferum*, with blue-green foliage and quite smooth stems. The flowers are mostly double and the seed heads are very attractive for use as winter decorations. Poppy flowers are also good for decoration, if, directly they are cut, the ends of the stems are placed in boiling water for about 30 seconds, to seal them. Flower buds that are just beginning to show colour should be selected and they will then last for several days in water. *P. somniferum* is best purchased in mixed packets, but a new variety, called *P.* 'Peaony-flowered Pink Beauty', is a superb form that has extra double, large, pink flowers, $2\frac{1}{2}$ feet in height.

Scabious is now available in a much wider range of colours, and produces vigorous plants with plenty of flowers right through the summer season. Growing on long stiff stems the

Helianthus

Shirley Poppies (*above*) are obtainable in a wide range of colours and varieties.

flowers range through many shades of pink, pale mauve, blue and dark maroon. A well grown plant should achieve a height of 3 to 4 feet, and a width of $1\frac{1}{2}$ feet. There is a dwarf form in similar colours growing to a height of 18 inches.

Stocks are really half-hardy annuals, which should be sown early, under glass and are well worth the extra trouble, because they do look so lovely in a border. The colours available include white, cream, yellow, pale copper, various pinks, mauves and purples. Giant Perfection is a good strain with strong-growing, free-flowering, branching plants up to 18 inches in height.

Sunflowers *(Helianthus)* are really more suitable in the lower growing forms for borders, than the ordinary giant variety, which are rather overpowering even as background annuals. They are not particularly attractive either, unlike the smaller varieties, which are obtainable in a wider colour range. Italian White, for instance, is 4 feet high and pale primrose with a dark centre. The Red has chestnut-brown flowers and the Dwarf Chrysanthemum type has extra double golden-yellow flowers with fringed petals and is only 3 feet high.

MIXED BORDERS

Preparation

A mixed border of biennials, summer bulbs, and herbaceous plants is probably one of the most rewarding features of the average sized garden. It has a long flowering period, provides flowers and foliage to cut for the house, and, once planted, requires the minimum of attention and outlay. One of the great advantages of herbaceous perennials is that they remain in position for several years. Provided the bed has been well prepared, as already explained, by double digging and the removal of all perennial weeds, it should only be necessary to hoe regularly between the plants to keep the ground open and destroy any surface weeds, with, in the autumn, a top dressing of compost lightly forked in. In the spring a dressing of bone meal, at the rate of 2 ounces per square yard should be hoed in. Throughout the season the plants should have their dead flowers removed as soon as they have faded and this will often result in a second crop of flowers later in the season. It is not advisable to remove their leaves until they lose colour. If it is

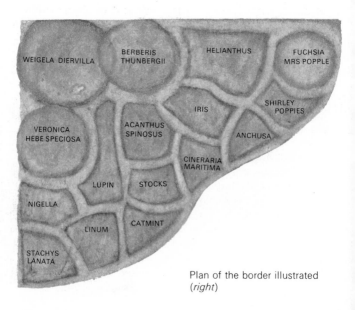

Plan of the border illustrated (*right*)

decided to move a plant to another position in the border, it should be left where it is until autumn, but a stick can be put against it with a label denoting the future site.

Choosing the site for a mixed border depends, naturally, on the size of the garden but ideally a mixed border should not be less than 4 feet wide by 12 to 16 feet long. If these measurements are impossible, it is better to plan a bed containing not more than six different types of herbaceous plant all of short or medium height with foliage that is tidy and green both before and after flowering, or it might perhaps be better to have specialist beds containing only one type of plant in each. Well coloured, long-flowering plants look good growing in narrow beds on either side of a path. A mixed border, where space allows, may be planned in crescent shape with perhaps one end curved out farther than the other. The varying widths will add to its attraction and, if the widest part of the border is raised, the general effect will be a great deal more interesting.

Careful attention will have to be given to the plants in a mixed border, as frequently rampant growers may suffocate other slower-growing plants

The mixed border is probably the most attractive and rewarding feature of the average sized garden.

Designing the border

The mixed border can be planned on a lawn, or have grass, brick or stone paths all round it, so that it may be viewed on all sides, although such a border does restrict the choice of plants, particularly the tall-growing ones, and tends to appear rather bare in winter. A background is useful as a wind-break and helps the general display, but house walls are not very practical for this purpose. New red brick kills so many of the plant colours, while painted brick or concrete walls make for difficulties when repainting becomes necessary. Few people are sufficiently fortunate to own a mellow, old brick or stone wall that can be used as a background to a border, and hedges and shrubs are most commonly used as a background to other plants and as a wind-break.

One thing which should be borne in mind when planning a border is that it is always better to be able to look along the border than straight at it. The position chosen should be open and sunny and, although facing south is the ideal position, there are many existing borders that face anywhere from south-east to

Method of staking tall plants

north-west, with great success. The exact position will depend on a number of other factors such as whether it is to be associated with a path, lawn or terrace, whether it is to be seen easily from the house, as a whole, or to be a surprise feature for visitors to the garden. It is possible to place the border on one or more levels in association with a paved path, or steps linking the whole.

If a hedge is planned a width of at least 18 inches should be allowed between the hedge and the plants at the back of the border. If this is not done then the hedge roots will be too close and will steal nourishment from the border plants. There must also be enough room to get between the hedge and the border to be able to tend the plants in the latter. Ideally a brick or stone path is the answer to this problem as there will be no weeds to encroach on the border, no grass to cut, no gravel to rake and no mud during bad weather. Herbaceous plants and summer bulbs are easy to grow, easily obtainable and do well in average soil, increasing in growth each year under normal conditions. Bolder efforts and experiments can follow with more experience and the old favourites are a wiser choice for the beginner.

The method of staking bushy plants (*left*), annuals (*centre*) and small clumps (*right*)

Other methods of staking plants

Selection table

The following list gives colour, height and flowering season, and used in conjunction with the suggestions for flowering shrubs previously given, it is intended to help the gardener make the final decisions about the contents of the mixed border.

Blue, mauve and violet flowers

Name	Height in feet	Flowering Period
Acanthus spinosus	2–4	July–September
Aconitum	3–5	July–August
panthus	3–4	Summer
Anchusa	1–3	May–August
Aquilegia	1½–3	May–July
Aster (Michaelmas Daisy)	1–5	August–October
Campanula	1–4	June–September
Cantananche caerulea	2	July–August
Canterbury Bell (blue)	2½	June–August

The Harts Tongue fern (*left*) and Rudbeckia (*right*) with Dwarf Michaelmas Daisies (bottom)

Delphinium	3–5	June–August
Echinops	1–2	June–September
Erigeron	1½	June–September
Iris (Flag)	2–3	May–June
Liantris	2½–3½	July–August
Limonium latifolium (statice)	2	July–September
Linum narbonense	1½	May–July
Lupin	2½–3	June–July
Nepeta	1–2	July–September
Platycodon	1	July–September
Phlox (also in other colours)	3–4	June–September
Salvia patens	2–3	June–August
Scabious	2–3	June–October
Stachys lanata	1	May–August
Thalictrum	4–5	May–August

Pink, Rose and Red Flowers

Achillea (red)	1½–2½	July–August
Alstroemeria ligtu hybrids	2–3	June–September
Anemone hupehensis	2–3	July–October

Lillium auratum and Paeony (*right*)

Aster (Michaelmas Daisy)	2–3	August–October
Astilbe	2–3	June–August
Bergenia	1	March–May
Chrysanthemum	2–5	August–October
Dianthus	1–1½	May–August
Dicentra	1–2	May–June
Geum	2	May–July
Gypsophila	2	June–July
Lupin	2–3	June–July
Lychnis coronaris	2–3	June–August
Lythrum	2–4	June–September
Paeony	2–3	May–June
Papaver (Oriental Poppy)	2–3	May–June
Phlox	3	June–September
Physostegia virginiana	1½–4	July–September
Polygonum	1–8	July–October
Sedum spectabile	1–3	August–September
Sidalcea	3	June–August

Yellow, Bronze and Orange Flowers

Achillea filipendulina	4–5	June–September
Alyssum saxatile	1	April–May
Anthemis tinctoria	2	June–August
Aquilegia	1–3	May–July
Aspodeline lutea	3–4	July–August

Sidalcea

(*Below*) *Viburnum davidii* and
(*centre*) *Campanula*
Gaillardia (*left*)

Chrysanthemum	2–5	August–October
Coreopsis	2–3	June–September
Digitalis	2–4	July–October
Gaillardia	2–3	June–August
Gazania splendens	1	Summer
Kniphofia	4–5	July–September
Lupin	2½–3	June–July
Potentilla	3	June–September
Ranunculus	1–2	May–June
Rudbeckia	2–5	July–October
Solidago	2–6	July–October
Trollius	2–3	May–July
Verbascum	2–6	June–September

White and Cream Flowers

Achillea clavennae	1	June–September
Asphodelus albus	2–3	May–June
Campanula	2–4	June–September
Delphinium	3–5	June–August
Dianthus	1–1½	May–August
Gypsophila	2	June–August
Iris (Flag)	2–3	May–June
Hesperis (Sweet Rocket)	2	May–June
Papaver	2–3	May–June
Phlox	3	June–September
Scabious	1½–3	June–October

Senecio laxifolius

Santolina chamaecyparissus

Euphorbia marginata

Crown Imperials are attractive when planted in groups but rarely seen these days. Their correct name is *Fritillaria imperialis.*

Bulbous plants

In addition to the above well-known herbaceous plants there are some bulbous subjects that look particularly attractive when grown in the mixed border. Crown Imperials for instance, are not seen very often, yet when planted in groups, 6 inches deep and 6 to 8 inches apart in September to November, the yellow or deep orange, bell-like flowers circling each stem, topped by a tuft of strap-like leaves, arouse great interest when they appear in May. *Fritillaria imperialis* is their correct name. They are quite hardy, but like an annual top dressing of well-decayed manure. Galtonia, or *Hyacinthus candicans,* is another beauty for the border. It is summer-flowering, growing to 3 feet with white flowers that grow in much the same manner as a spring-flowering hyacinth but on a larger scale, the waxy bells clinging to the tall stems with similar strap-like leaves. This plant is quite distinctive.

Acidanthera bulbs can be planted about 2 inches deep and 3 inches apart, from April onwards, and will flower in August to October. The flowers, white with a dark purple blotch and very fragrant, grow in a similar manner to those of Gladioli, but both their stems and flowers are more delicate than the latter. *Gladioli* are also useful subjects for the mixed border when planted in groups. Butterfly Gladioli are particularly recommended. A smaller type, with mottled throats in a very interesting colour range, they seem to blend with other flowers more happily than the larger flowered Gladioli.

The Kaffir Lily *(Schizostylis)* is a hardy bulbous and rhizomatous-rooted perennial and useful because it flowers in October and November, when the colour, pink or cerise, makes it outstanding among the late autumnal shades of most other flowers. It also lasts well as a cut flower.

All the summer-flowering bulbs can remain in the border during the winter, except the large flowered Gladioli, which must be lifted in November and stored until they can be re-planted in March. Butterfly Gladioli need not be lifted.

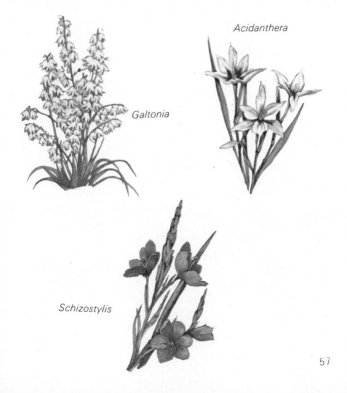

Acidanthera

Galtonia

Schizostylis

FOLIAGE PLANTS

Selection of plants

Plants grown for their foliage are very popular these days. They can be grown in mixed borders, but sometimes are even more effective if grown together in beds. A grey-foliaged bed can be very attractive even in winter, for many of these plants keep their leaves in winter and, if there is a need for a little more colour when the spring comes, a few annual flower seeds can be sown among the silvery permanent inhabitants that will give the annuals a wonderful background.

Stachys lanata keeps its velvety silver foliage in the winter and provides a good ground cover. In the spring it puts up shoots, with the grey buds followed in summer, by tiny purple flowers. Its height is never more than 15 inches and after flowering the stems can be cut off, to encourage the narrow leaves to increase the density of the grey ground cover. A slightly taller, grey, herbaceous plant which keeps its foliage is *Ballota*, which is easy to grow, evergreen, with shrubby growth. The small flowers are insignificant but silvery grey whorls grow round the arching stems, and the round velvet leaves can be cut in the autumn to dry for winter use in the house. *Senecio greyii* is a medium sized shrub, 2 to 3 feet high, which has silvery grey branches, and slightly darker, ovate leaves with a silvery back. The branches have graceful curves and the buds, in July, are silver-grey bunches. These open to bright yellow daisy-shaped flowers, which seem a garish touch on such a quiet elegant shrub. However, if these flowers are removed as soon as they have finished flowering the grey leaves will remain for the rest of the year. *Senecio cineraria* is another silver-foliaged plant, this time with deeply serrated leaves which are almost white. It looks lovely growing against darker coloured leaves, is quite hardy and can be grown in southern districts.

The Cotton Lavender *(Santolina)* is a small grey-green evergreen plant about eighteen inches high, which has feathery foliage, and makes an excellent edging plant. It can be clipped to a miniature hedge in the autumn and will shoot again in the spring to make a neat finish to the front of the border, or to paths, during the winter.

Ballota and (left)
Macleaya cordata

Hosta fortunei

Rheum palmatum

Hosta is usually grown for the foliage but it does have graceful sprays of bell-shaped flowers in July. There are many different varieties and (*right*) is *Hosta ventricosa*. There are also many varieties of Ivy and *Hedera dentata aurea* (*centre*) is one of the more attractive forms. (*Far right*) Lamb's Ears or *Stachys lanata*

Hosta has charming leaves, and is grown mainly for its foliage, although it does have flowers in July, which grow in graceful sprays with bell-shaped, mostly mauve flowers on one main stem. There are many different types of leaves that vary in size and the variegated ones are particularly attractive. The leaves of all the many varieties are ovate on single stems, the sizes ranging from five inches to ten inches with the length of the stem varying between three inches and eight inches.

The leaves are most important to the flower arranger and there are many varieties from which to choose. *Hosta albo marginata* has white-edged, green leaves and *H. crispula* is a larger form of marginata. *H. fortunei albo picta* has primrose yellow leaves edged with green, *H. fortunei* large glaucous leaves, *H. sieboldiana* large light blue-grey corrugated leaves and *H. undulata medio-variegata* prettily variegated wavy leaves. All these plants like a fairly shady position, and can be divided up every third year. A watch for slugs must be kept because they are particularly attracted by the tender leaves.

Hedera has a variegated form, *H. colchica dentata variegata*,

that has golden mottled leaves growing up to ten inches across. It is a very attractive sight in winter, especially when it is found growing against a wall or fence, and is perhaps more appreciated at that time of year rather than in the summer when it has all the summer-flowering climbers with which to compete.

Pampas Grass, although still considered a rather Victorian feature in a garden, is really a most decorative plant. It is at its best if given a small bed to itself on a lawn, or in a courtyard, where its silvery plumes will look very handsome indeed.

Cardoon *(Cynara cardunculus)* is another beautiful grey-leaved plant and is a perennial that can easily be grown from seed. It has very large, silvery, serrated leaves that can easily measure four feet in height and it bears tall, thistle-type, purple flowers in August. It is a very large handsome plant and the foliage will last the entire winter in most of the southern districts, shooting anew during the early spring.

Euonymus radicans variegata is an extremely attractive low-growing plant. It is very colourful when planted at the edge of a rock garden or in a trough or stone sink.

Zea mays are ornamental grasses that are very useful for flower arrangements and reach an average height of four feet. The leaves are all variegated, depending on the species for the colour. *Senecio cineraria* (*above right*) has silver leaves and is generally used as a background to the more colourful summer plants. (*Below right*) *Cortaderia argentea* is more commonly known as Pampas Grass.

The Ornamental Rhubarb *(Rheum palmatum)* is a hardy perennial foliage plant that needs plenty of space to accommodate its large purple-bronze leaves. Growing to a height of from four to six feet, it is a very striking plant and is especially attractive in a corner where it can spread itself undistorbed.

There are a number of hardy ferns that can be grown easily in odd corners of the garden such as on the top of walls. *Phyllitis scolopendrium* is the popular Hart's Tongue fern, and is a hardy evergreen one, six to eighteen inches high. The Hard Shield Fern is also a hardy plant and it has fronds up to three feet high. There is also the Sensitive Fern *(Onoclea sensibilis)* that is hardy, deciduous and two to three feet tall.

Zea mays japonica is classed as a half-hardy annual, ornamental grass, but its wide strap-like leaves are variegated silver and green and always make an impressive group, growing to a height of four feet. *Zea mays gigantea quadricolor* has a similar leaf form, striped white, yellow, green and rose, and reach 4 feet in height. The leaves of both types are useful for flower arrangement.

Euphorbia marginata (Snow-on-the-Mountain) a hardy annual, has pale green leaves, margined with white, and white bracts, and makes a pretty summer foliage plant. Another hardy annual, sometimes called Annual Poinsettia *(E. heterophylla)*, has vivid green branching foliage and each of the stems ends in a whorl of scarlet leaves. Both these annual euphorbias grow eighteen inches high.

There are also two climbing plants with outstanding foliage. One, *Humus lupulus* (Hop), is a hardy perennial climber, ten to fifteen feet in height, and is the commercial hop with its pale green hop flowers. It can become a very decorative camouflage for unsightly objects and grows very rapidly in summer, although it must be cut to the ground in autumn. The golden leaved form, *H. aurus*, is a decorative partner. There is also an annual Japanese Hop, *H. japonicus variegatus*, eight to ten feet high, that has an attractive green and white variegated foliage.

Bamboos are very attractive. Many of them have colourful stems, as well as variously shaped leaves. Some plants have square stems.

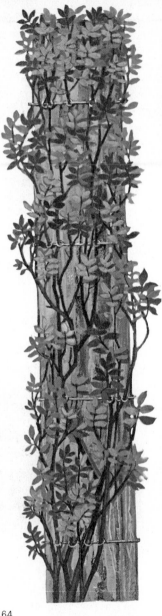

CLIMBING PLANTS

Climbing plants can be used in so many ways. There are all decorative plants, although some like the hops, have beauty mainly in their foliage, while others are more noted for their flowers. A climber recommended for the colour of its leaves in autumn is *Vitis thunbergii* (Vine) that has ornamental black fruits and large leaves that are richly coloured during the autumn. It can be trained to climb up a stout post, as well as against walls or buildings. *Vitis vinifera purpurea* has red leaves in summer, while in the autumn many of the leaves turn to purple, and the mixture of the two colours against a building is a very memorable sight indeed.

The annual climbers can be used to make a very effective camouflage for such things as unsightly sheds or other outbuildings. They can also be used against archways or pergolas during the time that the selected perennial climbers are settling in to start their permanent growth.

One of the better known of

Methods of training Climbing plants, (*left*) on a post and (*right*) training against a wall the annual climbers is Nasturtium *(Tropaeolum)*, that gives a wonderful show of colour for the minimum of effort. *T. spitfire* is a vivid bright red in colour and will, if planted where it can throw its fiery colour over fences or down banks, appear very dazzling in its visual impact. There are so many colours to choose from among the climbing nasturtiums, ranging from creamy yellows, through golds, oranges, to a deep coppery red, and they will all last well into the autumn. A close relation to the nasturtium is the Canary Creeper which has smaller yellow flowers. It is an annual climber that can be used where a more flamboyant climber is not required.

The Canary Creeper is often allowed to trail over shrubs, especially those which flower in winter and are devoid of flowers in summer.

Morning Glory *(Ipomaea)* should be placed in a warm sunny corner of the garden against a fence or wall and will require the support of twigs or string. Their flowers do not last more than a day, but they follow each other in such quick succession that one hardly notices their fading. *Ipomaea* are obtainable in blue, red, white, wine colour, and magenta but the blue, *rubro-caerulea praecox*, is perhaps the most beautiful colour of all the many varieties.

Cobea scandens, a half hardy annual, is an unusual climber, rather slow to germinate, but once it does, it grows rapidly to a height of ten to twelve feet. It will do well against a house wall in a sunny position sheltered from the wind. Some thin wires strained at intervals against and across the wall will provide a hold for its tendrils, which can be gently trained *along* the wires rather than *up*, to spread the coverage. The cup-like flowers on five-inch stems, are pale green in bud, but change on opening, first to pale mauve, then purple.

Jasminum nudiflorum (Winter Jasmine), a hardy climbing shrub, is a great delight in the winter, when it will clothe a wall with its starry, golden yellow flowers, which last from December until the spring. If picked in bud they will open well in the house. This jasmine seems to grow anywhere, but against a north wall the shoots grow longer. If these long

Jasminum nudiflorum

shoots are left on the shrub they will provide the best future flowering shoots. The shorter, more branching pieces will look better in the house, and cutting these will give about as much pruning as will be necessary.

For quick growth there is a climber known as Russian Vine *(Polygonum baldschua-nicum)*, which is popular because it has a sturdy vigorous growth in the summer and attains a height of up to twenty feet. It has small white flowers tinged with pink, growing in sprays along its stems, and these are good for dressing a shed or something similar, but too rampant for house or garage unless kept firmly under control. Nevertheless, it is an attractive and useful climber, especially as it flowers late in the year.

Vitis thunbergii is a vine that has ornamental black fruits and large richly-coloured leaves during the autumn. It can be trained up a post or a wall.

Another rather rampant grower is *Clematis montana rubens*, which has single pale pink flowers with yellow stamens. This flowers from May until July, and likes sun, but a close watch should be kept on its many tendrils and an endeavour be made to train these on horizontal wires such as with *Cobea scandens*. It is not desirable to let this clematis get under the roof tiles. All the clematis are attractive, although the *C. montana* is the speediest grower, and should have its old wood removed after flowering to keep it under control. The common purple Clematis *(C. jackmanii)* grows well and usually gives no trouble to the gardener. There is a variety called *C. tangutica* with smaller, lantern-shaped, yellow flowers, followed by silvery seed heads like balls of silky down. This should be cut down to within two feet of the ground in February, and will shoot again in the early spring, making an excellent climber for a garden arbour. It flowers in July and looks well in association with a climbing yellow rose such as Mermaid, which has single flowers and outstanding deeper yellow stamens, or the Banksian Rose with its clusters of double yellow flowers. Somehow the combination of climbing roses and clematis seems a particularly happy one. *C. rehderiana* is another clematis that likes to entwine itself in the branches of a

Clematis montana rubens

yellow climbing rose and has clusters of small, primrose yellow blossoms which are cowslip scented.

Clematis 'Nelly Moser' has large, single, pale mauve flowers striped with red which come out in June. This looks very attractive if grown with a red climbing rose as a supporting background. *C. orientalis* has four waxy flower petals, which are first of all green, then turn to yellow, and finally to orange, with sea-green fern-like foliage. It starts to flower at the beginning of July and often goes on flowering until November. *C. kermesina* has purplish-pink flowers and *C. jouiniana* has sprays of small white, lilac-tinted flowers from August to October.

The many varieties of clematis thrive best in a chalk or lime soil and like to have their roots shaded, perhaps by a wall or shrub and be able to climb into the sunlight. The stems of all clematis are very slender and tend to be brittle and they should be given a very firm support. Damage often occurs through accidental breakage caused by careless handling.

Clematis 'Nelly Moser' flowers during June.

A. slow grower, but well worth waiting for, is *Wisteria*. The most popular form is the Chinese Wisteria (*W. sinensis*), which has deep lilac flower spikes up to twelve inches long in May and early June. It likes a position in full sunlight against walls with a southern exposure or on pergolas, arbours, trellis, or scrambling over a tree. It should be pruned in July after flowering simply by shortening all the young shoots that are not required for extending branches, to within one inch of the base of the branch. Wisteria growing naturally over branches of a tree should not be pruned. All the varieties can be increased by layering immediately the plant has flowered.

Honeysuckles (*Lonicera*) are obtainable in great variety. Some are evergreen, some deciduous, and a number flower in winter and spring.

Passiflora caerulea is a half-hardy climber. It is usually known as the Passion Flower and has been given this name because it is said to bear, in its curiously formed flowers, all the instruments of the Crucifixion.

L. auro-reticulata has golden variegated foliage, almost ever-green, and flowers from June to August, while in contrast, *L. purpussii* is vigorous, winter-flowering and fragrant. *L. fragrantissima* has creamy-white flowers from December to March. *L. etrusca* is vigorous with creamy yellow flowers tinged with red and bears fragrant flowers in July. Honey-suckles like to have their roots in a shaded cool position, but the top growths should be in the sun. All the climbing honey-suckles can be increased by layering at almost any time of the year.

Passion Flower *(Passiflora caerulea)* is a beautiful and unusual half-hardy climber. The flowers are blue, white and green with long blue stamens. It is a slightly tender climber that grows best in a good ordinary soil mixed with a little decayed manure, and a slightly protected position against a south or south-west wall. It can be pruned in February by shortening all small shoots and it must be watered freely in dry weather, with applications of liquid manure once a month in summer. The base of the plant should be protected with straw or dry bracken in severe winter weather.

Wisteria

ROCK GARDENS

Types of garden

A rock garden, even if it is only on a small scale, can be a very interesting feature in a garden. The purpose of a rockery, as the rock garden is called, is to provide a setting for plants that normally flourish in a rocky setting. Most gardeners will not wish to grow rare alpine plants and will prefer the rock garden to provide a colourful and attractive scene. The rock garden can also be used to provide a break in the monotonous contour of an otherwise flat garden.

Care must be taken over the siting of the rockery and also in its construction. Most rock plants will require almost full sunlight, and a position beneath trees, where there is prolonged shade as well as often a continuous drip of rain from the branches, will only cause considerable damage.

The best position for a rockery is on a slope facing towards the south-east. The plants will not mind the cold and frosts will not harm them. If the rockery must be sited in an open space then it is a good idea to make the slopes that face to the south-east as gentle as possible and the slopes on the north side fairly steep.

Building a rock garden is essentially a simple process. A base must first be built to approximately the desired shape of

The construction of a rockery is a simple process. A central core of easily drained material must be built to roughly the desired shape of the final rockery. The rocks can be set in place in this base tilted inwards so that rain will pass to the centre. The stones support pockets of soil, added as the rockery is built.

the final rockery. This should be constructed of coarse stones or any other material that will give good drainage. The rocks can be set in place in this base and each should be tilted slightly inwards so that the rain will pass to the centre of the rockery. The stones should support large pockets of soil, which is added as the rockery is built up. The rockery should never be made of a mound of soil with the rocks inserted afterwards. Each rock should be very finely fixed in place as it is positioned.

The soil that is used in the rock garden should be varied to accommodate as wide a selection of plants as possible. Where there is an area devoted to plants that like a lime-free soil, this section of the garden should be built vertically, the pockets of the lime-free soil above one another. If this is done, there is no danger that lime from one pocket will seep down to a place intended for plants that hate a soil containing any lime. Plants which dislike lime are called calcifugous, while those which are quite happy in soils containing lime are calcicolous.

All plants will require a soil that contains plenty of grit and the plants will differ in their requirements of leaf-mould, peat, sand, ash or stone chippings. Most of the common plants like a gritty soil that contains some leaf-mould and a little lime.

Some of the more deep-rooted plants are probably better if set in position during the building of the rockery. The placing of smaller plants can be done afterwards.

Rock plants are not only those suitable for planting and sowing in a rock garden, but also those that will be at home on top of, or in the crevices of dry walls. walls built of rough stone using soil instead of cement, so that one can insert plants between the stone where they will grow and provide lovely patches of colour. These dry walls are most useful for dividing different levels in the garden, or raising flower beds.

On paving paths too, rock plants planted in between the paving stones look natural and gay. In courtyards, raised stone sinks planted with the really tiny plants, which can be seen to better advantage three or four feet from the ground, are both interesting and decorative. There are also a number of pottery garden bowls in different shapes and sizes on the market today and these are ideal for growing rock plants and miniature shrubs in many parts of the garden.

Selection of plants

Two well-known plants for dry walls in the spring are the yellow *Alyssum saxatile*, and *Aubrieta* in many shades of blue purple, purple-red, and rose. These growing in a dry wall or terrace, perhaps planted together with white Arabis and Iberis, make a wonderful show of colour in the early spring. The little double daisies *Bellis perennis*, especially the pinkish red 'China Pink' and the red 'Rob Roy', are charming rock plants, but they need dividing up fairly often. *Auriculas* are not really rock plants, but they are so fascinating with their rather glaucous grey-green leaves and unusual coloured flowers. They were first introduced in the sixteenth century, and having figured in many flower paintings of that period, are now coming back into favour. Surroundings of stone and rock seem to suit them and the efore their name is included in this list.

The Hardy Cyclamen require good drainage and shelter from wind but, in the rock garden or under stone walls facing north, and in garden bowls or sink gardens, their tiny flowers are charming. *C. atkinsii* in white, pink, or red with marbled foliage, flowers in February and March. *C. repandum* has

1 *Arabis* 2 *Primula auricula* 3 *Cotoneaster congesta* 4 Thrift

5 *Campanula* 6 *Edelweiss* 7 *Tulip kaufmanniana* 8 *Alyssum saxatile*

bright crimson flowers in April and May and *C. neapolitanum* pale pink flowers in autumn.

Campanula portenschlagiana does well in the chinks of a dry wall, and the dwarf hybrid Campanulas can be grown from seed obtainable in many shades from pure white to dark blue. *Primula denticulata* is a spring-flowering primula with pastel coloured flowers growing in whorls round erect 8 to 12 inch stems. *Polygonum affine* is a hardy rock plant with pink flowers from August to October and although only 6 to 9 inches high, it is rather rampant so it is wise to give it plenty of space. Thrift can be used as a good 'cushion' plant with pink, sometimes red, flowers and *Armeria juniperifolia* is another shorter type of Thrift 3 inches high with single flowers. The different varieties of Dianthus include *D. alpestris* and *D. neglectus*, which are pink and *D. petraeus*, which is white. The dwarf Aquilegia (*A. scopulorum*) is another unusual rock plant.

Many small bulbs are excellent when set in small clusters in pockets of soil. Such bulbs as *Muscari praecox alba*, with white flowers; and *Crocus chrysanthus* varieties, *Leucojum aestivum*, *Iris danfordiae*, *Scilla siberica*, *Leucojum vernum*, *Tulipa pulchella*, *Tulipa kaufmanniana* are all extremely attractive.

9 *Aubrieta* 10 *Bellis perennis* 11 *Cytisus kewensis*

12 Candytuft 13 *Aubrieta* 14 *Vinca*

Thyme, including Wild Thyme (*Serpyllum*), has hairy foliage and purple flowers and *T. albus* with white flowers and *T. carneus* with flesh coloured flowers and very fragrant leaves, are all creeping plants that are good for terraces and stone walls. They can all be treated as half-hardy annuals. The trailing creamy-white Broom *Cytisus kewensis* looks most attractive spreading over a rockery and *Pernettya pumila* is another dwarf trailing plant with pink and white berries. *Cotoneaster microphylla* is a trailing evergreen shrub with scarlet berries for walls or rockeries, while *C. congesta* has dwarf growth.

Sempervivum (Houseleeks) are hardy succulent perennials that grow rosettes of fleshy dark green leaves, their points tipped with purple-brown. They look very attractive in groups on flagged paths or terraces as well as on steps and dry walls. *Sedum reflecum,* usually known as Stonecrop, is another tough little plant that can be grown easily on paths, terraces, walls, and in stone sinks. *Euphorbia polychroma*, with prostrate stems covered with small grey leaves terminating in bright, lime yellow bracts in early spring, is a hardy perennial.

Sedum spectabile (left), Primula denticulata (centre) and *(right) Sempervivum reginae-amaliae*, the hardy perennial houseleek

Edelweiss (*Leontopodium alpinum*) is another hardy perennial that is easily grown from seed and produces grey, velvety, narrow leaves with paler grey, narrow, petalled flowers. This is the Edelweiss from the European mountains but it seems just as much at home in an English rockery. *Iris reticulata*, the dwarf 6 inch purple and yellow Iris, will bloom in February, and *Narcissus bulbocodium* (Hoop Petticoat Daffodil) is yellow, flowers in April, and is 6 inches tall. The white, red and yellow *Tulipa kaufmanniana*, also 6 inches tall, blooms in March and the trailing variety, Bowler, of *Vinca* (Periwinkle) has dark, pure blue flowers early in the year. *Ixia maculata*, with narrow pointed leaves, has orange and yellow flowers in spring.

The dwarf fuchsia has pretty foliage as well as little fairy flowers on wiry stems while *Epimedium robrum* has attractive mahogany-tinted leaves. All these, and a large number of other hardy annuals of low growth will help to fill a rockery, walls, sinks, courtyard, terraces and paths. All rock garden plants will have to be inspected regularly, to ensure that they are not being overcrowded or overcrowding their neighbours.

Iris reticulata, the dwarf iris (*left*) blooms in February. (*Centre*) the small *Cyclamen neapolitanum* and (*right*) *Arabis caucasica*

Easily grown plants will awaken a child's interest in gardening.

A CHILD'S GARDEN

Choice of plot

If it is planned to set aside a small part of the garden as a children's garden, they must be given a fair start by giving them a piece of ground in a good open position with soil in reasonable condition, already, perhaps, containing a rose tree. This could be a pretty Floribunda rose, for example, for Floribundas have a long flowering period and are the right size for small fingers. The gift of one or two Sweet Williams, Canterbury Bells, and Wallflowers would also help to provide a start in horticulture.

A dark gloomy patch of ground, well out of sight, which has weeds, stones and snails for company is not going to appear very prepossessing. Children do not have the patience of adults, and are liable to get bored with gardening if they do not see pretty speedy results for their labour.

Seeds of easily grown hardy annuals are usually greatly appreciated. Such plants as Nasturtiums, Candytuft and

Larkspur will grow quickly and even a row of runner beans could be given to the young gardener. This provides the additional attraction for them of selecting a means of support for them such as pea sticks, or poles and string, the choice depending on the capabilities and age of the child. The flower buds will come first, then the scarlet flowers, followed by the tiny beans, and this keeps the interest alive until the beans are ready to pick for the pot, which is a really exciting moment. Lettuces, and radishes too, are easy and reasonably quick to grow.

In this way small children can be taught how to thin out, hoe, weed, and dig. They can be given smaller copies of the same tools, and taught how to clean their tools before putting them away. If it is possible, seed catalogues can be given to them in the winter so they can make their choice of seeds to order for the following year, although judicious pruning of the resultant list will probably be necessary. The difference between hardy annuals, biennials, and perennials can be explained. Some biennials could be sown in July for flowering the following year if they are interested, and probably tidying up in autumn will appeal more than weeding in the summer.

It is essential not to kill any initiative on the part of children to experiment with plants and seeds.

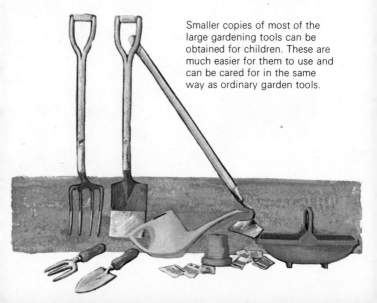

Smaller copies of most of the large gardening tools can be obtained for children. These are much easier for them to use and can be cared for in the same way as ordinary garden tools.

Other attractions

According to the size of the young gardener's plot and the age and sex of the gardener, the manufacture of nesting boxes, bird tables or perhaps a simple bench or seat, might be so timed as to fit in with the school carpentry class. A small garden can be designed to include one or more of these items quite easily and they often maintain interest in the duller times of the year. The family Christmas tree, always supposing that this is a rooted one, of course, might be nurtured back to health and strength after its duty in the house, in the garden of one of the younger members of the family. Combined with this is subsequent excitement of digging it up again the following Christmas.

If there are young daughters in the family, and there is a local flower show in the district, it might interest them to enter the children's flower arrangement class. Judging by the number of entries that these classes are now receiving at the shows they

Candytuft (*Iberis umbellata*)

Nasturtium

Radish

are becoming more and more popular each year, and the arrangements are usually of a very high standard indeed.

No doubt the whole of the garden will be viewed with an eye to using some of your flowers and foliage, but, as the materials do not have to be grown by the exhibitor in flower arrangement classes, this is permissible by the judges, if it is permissible by you. It is better for your own peace of mind, no doubt, if at least fifty per cent comes from the child's own garden and the child will probably feel far more satisfied with the results.

An uncrowded arrangement is generally far more effective than a large amount of flowers and foliage, and a few interesting leaves will be a greater improvement than more flowers. A number of schools now have flower arrangement on their curriculum, which is usually enjoyed by the school children and results in even more of them wishing to grow flowers and foliage of their own choice.

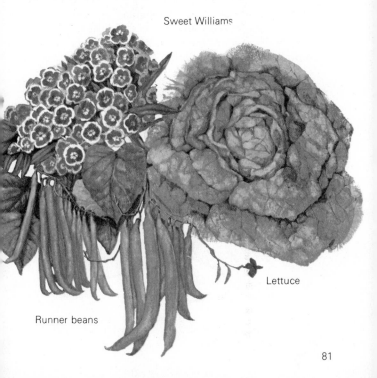

Sweet Williams

Lettuce

Runner beans

THE GARDEN IN WINTER

In the very late autumn one begins to appreciate the winter shrubs and flowers which provide interest during this drab, most empty time of the year, followed by the earliest of the spring plants in January. Somehow the foliage and flowers that appear at this bleak period are valued far more than the largesse of the summer garden. There is time to appreciate progress and one snowdrop often matters more than a whole bed of annuals. The unfolding flowers of the *Mahonia bealyii* at Christmas seem almost a miracle, while the petals of that winter-flowering tree, the *Prunus subhirtella autumnalis rosea*, pale pink against a pale blue winter sky, seen from any time during November to April, are quite breathtaking. The leaves of the *Tellima* begin to turn a fiery crimson in October. This has graceful stems with small pale green flowers in June, which assume a soft pinkish tint as they reach maturity, then the leaves start to turn in September until by October they are wholly red, and remain red throughout the winter months looking from a distance like patches of brilliantly coloured flowers in the border. These bright leaves are also invaluable for flower arrangements during the winter.

*Prunus subhirtella
autumnalis rosea*

Eranthis

Bergenia

Snowdrops

Bergenia starts to change the colour of its leaves in November and *B. delavayi* and *B. purpascens* are especially recommended for the effect they give throughout the 'dead' season of the year.

At the beginning of January the *Helleborus corsicus* starts to open its pale green clusters of flowers, which will continue until the end of May. It is a handsome plant that reaches about three feet in height and the contrast between the pale green, rather waxy looking petals and the leathery looking trifoliate leaves that are a darker brownish-green, is very striking. Two more *Helleborus* come out in January, *H. foetidus* and *H. kochi*. The former has pale green flowers that are rimmed with maroon, and dark green leaves while the latter opens buds of a very delicate pale yellow-green, almost primrose in colour.

Daphne laureola is an evergreen shrub that bears un-spectacular green flowers that have a noticeable scent towards the end of a winter's day. *Daphne mezereum* has white and purple flowers and also starts to fill the air with fragrance in January and somehow this fragrance on a dreary day seems more wonderful than any scent of the summer. *Stachyurus praecox* is a winter shrub which is hung with ropes of cream bells during the month of February and has reddish bark that enhances the value of the colour even more.

Mahonia japonica

Arbutus unedo or Strawberry Tree (*right*)

Ilex aquifolium

Japonicas are really spring flowering shrubs, yet *Japonica aurora* always starts to show the colour of its orange goblets from November onwards. The Viburnums are very welcome in the winter months and *Viburnum fragans* is one of the earliest to open, often starting in November. *V. burkwoodii* flowers in sheltered districts in November until April and May and *V. carlesii*, the Korean Guelder Rose, is a very fragrant variety.

The winter-flowering honeysuckles, which are also fragrant and so pleasant in winter, are very useful shrubs indeed. In particular, *Lonicera fragrantissima*, about six feet high and a semi-evergreen, is very commonly grown. This shrub bears creamy flowers.

Clematis balearica (*C. alycina*) is a winter-flowering Clematis that is not showy, but neat and attractive with dark bronzed foliage. This shows up the creamy-green, bell-like flowers very well indeed. They are blotched inside with a mahogany colour.

Clematis balearica

Pulmonaria officinalis

Erica carnea

Winter is the time when *Elaeagnus pungens aurea* flaunts its bright yellow and green variegated leaves and *Garrya elliptica* catkins hang their silvery, green length against the darker green of their leathery leaves. A variegated holly tree (*Ilex variegata*), which has leaves splashed with silver or gold, certainly brightens up the garden during the winter months, as does *Cornus alba* 'Weston Birt' which has polished, bare, bright coral stems. Another shrub that associates well with the *Cornus* is *Leycesteria formosa* which has beautiful smooth sea-green stems and wine coloured, graceful hanging bracts, carrying cream coloured flowers. In autumn these turn to wine coloured berries in the bracts while in winter the bare, green branches are welcome against the bright red of the Cornus stems.

Erica carnea can be grown in pink drifts, either in the rock garden or as a ground cover, with *carnea* 'Springwood White' looking like mounds of snow alongside it. *Iris histrioides* flowers in January and February and *Iris reticulata* in March. *Iris stylosa*, which is erratic in its flowering habits, sometimes starts to flower in late September and sometimes waits until December before showing its delicate pale mauve flowers.

Daphne mezereum and Cornus
alba 'Weston Birt' (right)

These only last a day, but, if picked in bud, are well worth taking into the house even for this brief period. The Periwinkle (*Vinca major*) produces clear blue flowers in winter and will make a flat carpet under any dormant summer shrubs. The Variegated Periwinkle with its cream and green leaves also makes a neat and tidy ground cover.

Iris foetidissima with sword-like foliage and bright orange berries, is good for winter colour and, in its striped variegated form, for indoor decoration. The tall *Phormium tenax* (New Zealand flax) reaches 5 feet and also has sword-like leaves of soft green and purple, which makes a bold clump among evergreens.

Chimonanthus fragrans has been mentioned earlier as has *Hamamelis mollis*. Both these are scented shrubs that flower without their leaves and a tiny sprig of either taken into the house will scent a whole room.

These winter-flowering shrubs are best planted near to a path or house, where they can be fully appreciated.

Viburnum carlesii

Chimonanthus praecox

Hamamelis molis

88

Very soon after Christmas the first small snowdrops begin to make their appearance. The ordinary snowdrop, *Galanthus nivalis*, is always the first to be seen, usually in double form, for although the single *G. nivalis* is prettier, it comes after the double. The next type to show is *G. elwessi*, a large flowered single, which is distinct and beautiful, with snowy-white globular flowers and inner segments marked with rich emerald green. The *Eranthis* (Winter Aconite) is also showing about January. *E. hyemalis* with flowers of bright yellow is good for growing under trees and in moist situations, while *E. tubergenii* 'Glory' which flowers a little later, has larger flowers of deep, rich yellow tinged with bronze and sweetly scented.

The winter-flowering Cyclamen are very welcome in February and March. *C. atkinsii album* is pure white with a red eye and marbled leaves while *C. atkinsii roseum* has soft rose-pink flowers and marbled foliage also. The beauty of these exquisite flowers at this time of year, with their perfect leaves, is yet another wonder of the winter garden.

Iris foetidissima has sword-like foliage and bright orange berries and is very useful for indoor decoration.

The leaves of *Arum italicum pictum* are out in November and will last all the winter. The short-stemmed spear-shaped leaves of this plant are most beautifully marbled with white and grey and they will make a very attractive indoor arrangement especially with flowers of the *Helleborus corsicus*. These pale green flowers against the dark green of the leaves with their light veining are delightful, but both the flowers and the leaves should be given at least six hours to float in a bowl of cold water in a cool place before they are arranged in a vase.

The Common Pulmonaria or Lungwort (*Pulmonaria officinalis*) starts to open its blue and pink flowers, which grow on 9 inch stems, towards the end of January. In February *P. saccharata* has flowers that are the same blue and red colours, but these are followed by attractive bristly, white-blotched leaves, which have a great foliage effect. *P. rubra*,

Iris stylosa

Arum italicum pictum

Helleborus corsicus

also February flowering, has pink flowers and plain, fresh green leaves. All the varieties are very easily grown in most soils providing they are given the correct amount of sun or shade. They can be increased by division during the spring or autumn.

In winter some of the most richly coloured foliage plants to grow in the garden are the variegated Kales, including the Flower Kale, and the new Osaka Kale. None of them are edible and they are all grown for their appearance alone, which gets more attractive as the winter advances. The winter frosts tend to emphasize the carmine-rose leafy rosettes of the Osaka until they resemble giant double flowers. The Kales can all be bought as seeds, for planting as hardy annuals in white, red, or mixed packets, but Osaka is only obtainable in one colour, carmine-rose. These plants can be placed at random almost anywhere in the garden and their colours are quite remarkable in the effect that they have. The red in particular are most useful when cut for the house.

Anemone blanda are particularly lovely when planted in mixed drifts and allowed to naturalize. They will appear each year in patches of blue.

THE GARDEN IN SPRING

By March the spring flowers make their appearance, and the gardening season really commences. Nowadays gardeners are becoming more bulb-minded because they realize how much wider a variety can be obtained, how easy the average bulb is to grow, and the fact that many of them can be planted in the autumn, then left in place thereafter, to increase by their own efforts.

The bulbs selected and planted by the gardener will then appear in subsequent springs in troughs, flower beds, or borders as the gardener begins the busy season of sowing the half hardy annuals, planning the annual border and applying bonemeal or any other fertilizers as well as countless other tasks. The spring bulbs, both those that were lifted and stored during the previous summer, and any new ones that were purchased, should have been planted in November and December, and results are now eagerly awaited.

Fritillaries were not grown very much a few years ago but have recently gained in popularity. They are attractive, interesting, and of an unusual colour and new varieties are constantly appearing.

It is possible to raise Fritillaries from seed, but this is a slow process often taking several years, and a greenhouse is a necessity, so that it is generally quicker to buy the bulbs, perhaps a dozen or so at a time, and thus build up a collection. So much of the beauty of Fritillaries is inside the hanging flower that they are seen at their best if planted above ground level, in a raised bed, on a shady bank, a sink garden, or a trough. *F. pallidiflora* has creamy flowers that are spotted inside with reddish brown and *F. meleagris saturnus* has large, pinkish, chequered flowers. *F. citrina* is only about 6 inches in height with dainty, citron yellow flowers tinged with green,

The best of the Fritillaries to cultivate is (*below*) the Snake's Head or Chequered Fritillary, *F. meleagris*.

while *F. ruthenica* in contrast has 2 foot stems, and brownish petals with a pale green lining, although the average height of the stem of Fritillaries is only 15 inches.

Polyanthus come into flower at this time and it is interesting to see what varieties can be obtained from the mixed seeds planted the previous summer as biennials. These are extremely easy plants to raise and will give such wonderful colour variety in the spring, that it is more exciting to grow them in a mixture, although one should not omit to label the colours that are particularly admired, for reference after the flowers have died down, for it is very doubtful that each individual colour will be remembered without the gardener having the flower as a guide. If some twigs are inserted between the polyanthus plants and then black cotton tied in a criss-cross fashion from twig to twig, this will form an unseen barrier against birds who find the small buds simply delicious.

After the plants have flowered, they should be lifted in order to make way for the summer bedding plants. If they are to be retained for subsequent years, as is usually the case, they should be divided at this time and planted in some good soil in a not too prominent part of the garden until the following autumn.

Even if the site in which the polyanthuses are being grown is not required for other plants during the summer, they should be lifted from their site. If they are left too long without being moved, they will become 'woody' in appearance and there will

Polyanthus

Vinca major has large round flowers of lavender-blue which open in April and May.

be a deterioration in the number of flowers and the length of the flower stems.

A real sign of spring in the garden is the appearance of the crocus. This is a hardy little bulbous plant that makes a very attractive edging to a mixed border or can be grown on a rockery or among the grass.

In addition to the well-known garden crocuses which occur in various shades of white, yellow, mauve and purple, there are a number of wild crocuses that can be planted, especially in a rock garden. The Early crocus (*C. imperati*) is in bloom in January and is buff outside and purple inside. *C. vernus* is the Spring crocus and has pale mauve flowers in March, while the Cloth-of-Gold crocus (*C. susianus*) has gold flowers, also in March.

Anemones are lovely in April, *Anemone blanda* in particular. Planted in mixed drifts then allowed to naturalize, the pale blue flowers with their delicate serrated foliage make a haze of soft colour. This foliage quietly disappears at the finish of the flowering season, only to reappear in a sheet of blue the following year, when they have almost been forgotten. There is a dark blue form, *A. blanda atrocoerula*, and a dazzling white, *A. blanda bridesmaid*. Mixed single De Caen Anemones are good spring plants and should be planted from November,

The ideal method of growing spring-flowering Crocuses is to naturalize them where they can form drifts of colour every year.

at intervals until late spring, in clumps for the cheerful patches of colour they give, red, blue, mauve, white and pink. They are useful for cutting too, and last well in winter.

Alliums are another useful family for spring and summer, which like so many others, should be planted in November. *A. aflatunense* has dense spherical umbels of purple-lilac, flowering from the end of May and reaching a height of about $2\frac{1}{2}$ feet. *A. elatum* flowers at the same time but is slightly taller, with broad shining green leaves, and rose-lilac umbels.

It is well worth growing some of the more unusual tulips, such as the Viridiflora type in particular. The best of these hybrids are *Tulipa viridiflora*, all with the sturdy green petals of that variety, on which are superimposed shades of yellow, pink, and white. These are a new, unusual series of great artistic and garden merit, and among them is particularly recommended *Artist* which is pinky-terracotta and green, passing entirely to green as the blooms fade. *Formosa* is a uniform greenish-yellow throughout, with again a characteristic marking of green on the outside of the petals, one of the latest to bloom.

The Botanical Tulip species are fine for the rock garden. Most of them have large flowers and short stems. Many of the species carry several flowers on one stem such as *T. praestans*, from Bokhara, which bears three to four bright orange-red flowers on one stem in early April. A fairly sheltered situation is advisable for all the multi-flowered types. *T. praestans wanenburg* produces three or four vermilion flowers on a stem, and *T. tarda* (Dasystemo) carries in April bunches of three to six star-shaped yellow and white flowers, perfect for a sunny position on the rockery.

The early-flowering double Tulips look charming massed in groups in the border, or filling smaller beds, particularly when used in mixed colours. They are robust, with large double flowers in good colours of white, yellow, peach, pink, orange, purple and scarlet, and the sturdy, medium height stems stand up to the spring gales in April much better than the taller, single tulips. The later-flowering double tulips,

(*Top left*) *Sparaxis tricolor* with three of the varieties of Allium, the Flowering Onion, (*from top to bottom*) *A. moly*, *A. ostrowskianum*, and *A. karataviense*

Darwin Tulips (*above*) flower in May.

which follow the early doubles at the beginning of May, are even more handsome because they are taller with even larger flowers.

It is wise to plant these double tulips in groups of five or six either against the foot of a wall or with a shrub background and there, until they start to increase in number, they can make a permanent home. When they have increased sufficiently it is as well to dig them up and store them until the autumn, when they can be replanted about 5 to 6 inches apart at least.

The large double tulips often produce blooms that are 6 to 8 inches in diameter so that care should be taken to see that the bulbs are planted sufficiently far apart to allow for this. Mount Tacoma is a late double tulip of great distinction, opening like a white Chinese paeony to a flower of immense size that lasts a long time on the plant, and also in water if cut. Red Ace is a sport of Mount Tacoma and a similar size, but a deep glowing red. Golden Lion is a deep gold and Orange Triumph a soft orange-flushed brown, with a narrow edging and flowers, when fully open, measuring 8 inches in diameter. Lilac Perfection is bluish lilac, and there are many more to choose from.

It would be impossible to describe all the different types of tulips that are available but to mention a few, there are the Early Single Tulips (April-flowering), Mendel Tulips (Mid-season), Multi-flowered Tulips (Branch flowering) and Fringed, Parrot, Rembrandt and Bizarre Tulips, all flowering in May.

Double Tulip

Cottage Tulip (*above*) and Botanical Tulip (*right*)

Cytisus albus, the early White
Spanish Broom

The Iris family are a splendid help in the spring, especially the Dutch Iris which bloom in a great variety of colour, and colour combinations, from May onwards. These are followed into flower about a fortnight later by the first of the Spanish Iris, which are slightly smaller in growth but make valuable cut flowers, especially during this time of year which is rather between flowering seasons. There is also very good colour in the Spanish Iris and, if they are planted in a mixture, they will make a very good show indeed in the garden. These Iris should be planted during the month of October, and be re-planted about every third year, although in the meantime they can be left in the ground to look after themselves.

There is another spring-flowering Iris that is rarely grown these days and may not appeal to everyone. This is the Widow Iris, *Hermodactylus tuberosus,* which has sword-shaped leaves and delicate lime green and black petals with a sweet scent. Although they are not often seen growing, they have been sold in Covent Garden for the past twenty years as cut flowers.

Lupins begin to flower in May. The Russell Lupins in particular are highly recommended for their wonderful colour range and produce the finest forms of flowers. These

The British Guelder Rose
(*Viburnum opulus*) is usually
grown in its sterile form in
which the flower heads are
transformed into white balls,
from which it gets its popular
name of Snowball Tree.

can either be grown from seed, as biennials, and sown in the
summer for flowering the following year or bought as young
plants in the autumn which means that by the spring they will
be sturdy young plants that will produce good spikes of mixed
colours flowering in May onwards. Even if young plants are
bought to start the Lupin collection, it is still a good idea to
grow a few seeds. A mixed packet of Russell Lupin seed will
give about two dozen seedlings, with a good choice of colours.
Lupins seldom come true to colour, therefore taking a chance
with a mixture like this often produces very interesting
varieties.

Lupin plants increase in size every year so it may be
necessary to divide them every second year, according to
their size. This is best done during the late autumn, and each
flowering spike should be cut off as it starts to die and before it
goes to seed. If this is done it will encourage fresh buds to
form and thus prolong the flowering season of the plant for as
long as it is possible.

Ideally, spring-flowering bulbs should be left until they have died down completely and the foliage has turned brown. If they occupy a prominent position they should be lifted and replanted elsewhere.

May-flowering shrubs will bring more colour to the scene, such as *Weigela praecox,* and the early White Spanish Broom (*Cystisus albus*) one of the earliest of the Brooms to flower. The pale-green balls of the Guelder Rose (*Viburnum opus sterile*) gradually turn to white at this time while Wisteria, the yellow *Laburnum vossii*, which can be obtained either as a bush or in standard form, and the spring-flowering honeysuckle *Lonicera syringantha*, a loose-growing shrub with scented rosy-lilac flowers, are all attractive.

Sparaxis are a type of Cape bulbs, which have narrow leaves and flowers usually two or three on each slender stem, that provide a gay mixture of colours. They are equally lovely growing in the rock garden, or in groups in the border and should be planted in the autumn and given a sunny position in well-drained soil, with some protection, such as dried bracken, in frosty weather. They will then naturalize themselves in all but the coldest regions or places with very heavy soil.

When bulbs are finally lifted they should be inspected for disease and rubbed clean of any earth that is clinging to them before they are stored in a clean box in a dry place, ready for autumn planting.

During their period of growth spring bulbs should need no stakes and, in fact, they should need little or no attention until the flowers have faded. After this the problem arises as to whether to leave the bulbs where they are in the garden or to lift them immediately.

Ideally the bulbs of spring flowers should be left until they have died down completely and the foliage has turned brown. By this time the roots and leaves will have served their purpose and formed a new bulb ready for growth the following year. If bulbs have been grown for spring display in a prominent position and must be removed, then the alternatives are to scrap them completely or carefully replant them in another part of the garden.

If bulbs are being saved for subsequent years they should be lifted from the ground when the foliage dies down. The bulbs must be rubbed clean of earth and stored in a box in a dry place until they can be planted out in the autumn.

THE GARDEN IN SUMMER

When June starts the summer annuals begin to show buds and a number of the earlier perennials are already out. Among these are Day Lilies, Digitalis, Aquilegias and the Giant Ranunculus which if planted from December until April at successive intervals will flower from May until July.

During the three mid-summer months so many lovely flowers come into bloom that is is difficult to know how many to suggest. It would perhaps be more helpful to give the names of the lesser known types or varieties, as one of the many

Old wood must be cut out of shrubs and a sharp pair of secateurs should always be used.

pleasures of gardening is to be able to have in one's own garden some of the plants that neighbours and friends have not yet grown. This list will not necessarily be in the order of blooming, but will be plants that flower between June, July and August. All these plants will not of course automatically discard their blooms at midnight on 31 August and many will continue, while others will have a second flowering season. If there has been a cold, wet summer, which is not unknown, a plant that should have been at its best in July may have misunderstood the season and postponed its opening until September. However, although pessimism appears to be a characteristic trait among gardeners, this list is compiled with a view to perfectly normal summers.

Acanthus spinosus is an attractive plant with stiff 4 foot high spikes of purplish-green and white flowers, and rather large, shiny, dark green leaves, deeply cut and spiny. It is a native of Mediterranean lands and likes well-drained soil and a sunny position. The flower spikes dry well for winter flower arrangements.

A clean cut should be made above a bud, joint, or another shoot on the same branch.

Alchemilla mollis (Ladies Mantle), with attractive soft green leaves and branching stems of pale green tiny flowers, makes a useful colour-divider in the border, as well as a most charming background for almost any cut flowers in the house. It increases rapidly and should be divided every other year, but the plants make a welcome gift, so there is no need to fear a glut in one's own garden! Not fussy about soil or position – it is equally happy in sun or partial shade.

Anchusa azurea has flowers similar to the forget-me-nots, but is much taller (3 to 5 feet) with large basal leaves of rough, dark green. It is attractive to bees and the bright blue flowers make a lovely colour background for the mixed border.

Anthericum (St Bernard Lily) look at their best growing in clumps and the small white open flowers grow in spikes, with sword-like leaves. It likes rich moist soil and is a good plant to grow with shrubs.

Arisaema candidissimum has white, sometimes pink, arum-like flowers, and likes sunny borders, and an occasional application of liquid manure in summer. The height is 1½ feet.

Asphodeline lutea is a taller plant (3 to 4 feet) with tufted basal leaves, and yellow, fragrant flowers growing up the tall stems, for which most soils are suitable.

Astilbe fanal has bronze leaves and dark red plumes of flowers. *A. davidi* also has bronze foliage, and magenta flowers, growing to 3 to 4 feet. The Astilbes are useful, undemanding plants as long as they are given partial shade and plenty of water. There are also several dwarf varieties available for the rock garden.

Penstemon bears tall spikes of flowers (*left*) and *Eremurus*, the Foxtailed Lily, (*right*) is attractive, but rarely seen.

St. Bernard Lily (*left*) and
Lobelia fulgens (*right*)

Astrantia is an interesting plant, again not often seen, and yet easy to grow. The flowers have cushion centres growing in groups on the tops of the stalks and the leaves are lobed. *A. major* has white or pink flowers and both these colours are intermixed with green. The height is about 2 feet.

Campanula persicifolia is an ordinary Campanula, yet seldom seen in the pure white form. The glossy foliage is evergreen and the basal leaf 'mats' make useful ground cover.

Delphiniums are available in a tremendous variety, both single and double, in heights from 1 foot to 6 feet, and colours from white to purple. *Delphinium zalil*, which is a yellow one few people know about, has yellow flowers that are produced in rather thin spikes from 2 to 3 feet high, and require staking. It is a native of Persia, and the only way at present of obtaining plants is to grow them from very scarce seed as a hardy perennial. The other little-grown Delphinium is *D. nudicaule*, a dwarf (1½ feet) scarlet-flowered variety from California, that may also have to be grown from seed.

Dianthus (Pinks) are another large genus of annual and perennial plants and the selection of most of them can be left to individual choice. *D. plumarius* is the original cottage pink from which the modern garden Pink has been derived. Most varieties are fragrant, in a wide range of colours, and all may be raised from seed. *D. doris* is a scented bright, salmon-pink Dianthus, which is easy to please, and *D. purity* has large double pure white flowers, with the fragrance of cloves.

Dicentra (Bleeding Heart) is a dainty plant with fern-like foliage. The most graceful of the species is *D. spectabilis* which has heart-shaped flowers nearly an inch long, drooping in arching sprays. The flowers are either white or rose-coloured.

Echinops (Globe Thistle) are rather stately plants, which are particularly useful for the back of the border as they range

Salpiglossis sinuata

Echinops ritro

in height from 3 to 6 feet. *E. ritro* is one of the best, with divided leaves that are spineless and cobwebby above and downy beneath, and blue or steely-blue flowers at a height of 3 to 4 feet.

Eremurus (Foxtailed Lily) is a seldom seen, but very attractive flower. *E. robustus* has erect peach-coloured spikes of flowers up to 3 feet long, and bright green strap-like leaves. This plant is a native of Asia and not completely hardy, but this is a risk worth taking. The danger period seems to be in the spring when new growth begins, and some covering should be given

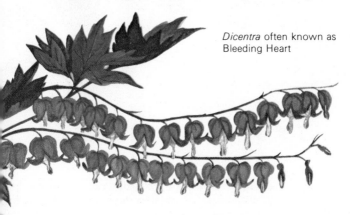

Dicentra often known as Bleeding Heart

at that time. It should be planted in a sunny position and not disturbed for at least three years.

Erigeron are rather similar to summer-flowering Michaelmas Daisies, and are of robust growth, remaining in bloom almost without a break from June to October. The stalks should be cut down after the first flush of flower in June or July, and the plants will soon flower again. Their average height is $1\frac{1}{2}$ to 2 feet and the colours range from pale mauve to violet-mauve and bright and deep pink to deep violet-blue.

Galtonia grows like a giant hyacinth although the white bells are more widely spaced along the 3-foot stems. It flowers from July to August. It is not fussy about soil, and can remain undisturbed for years. *G. candicans* grows to a height of 3 feet while *G. princeps* has a touch of green on the buds and is a lighter looking plant, 2 feet in height.

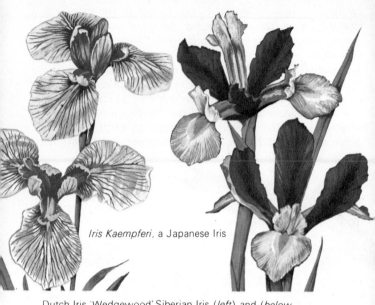

Iris Kaempferi, a Japanese Iris

Dutch Iris 'Wedgewood' Siberian Iris (*left*) and (*below right*) a variety of Bearded Iris 'Lady Mohr'

Gypsophila, a dainty small-flowered plant, can be a great help in the garden as a 'separator' between the rather solid growth of so many other plants. It can be grown as a hardy annual, in white, pink, or deep pink at a height of 1 foot. It is useful for cutting as well.

Iris germanica, or June-Flowering Iris, like lime and should have some broken chalk or mortar-rubble added to the soil. They should be given a sunny position in the garden and divided about every three years. They look charming in a mixture of colours in a raised bed, but are not very attractive together with other plants. One of the prettiest varieties is *I. germanica* 'Blue Shimmer' which is ivory white dotted with clear blue. *I. g.* 'Staten Island', gold and maroon, and Silver City, a soft grey-blue, are also lovely, but there is such a wide range of colours from which to choose that it is better to make a personal decision with the aid of a catalogue.

Kniphofia (Red Hot Poker) have changed during the past few years, and there are some different colourings in the range.

Modesta is white with rose tips and 2 feet high, while Samuels Sensation is 4 feet high, a very large coral red, developing a slight buffish margin at the base of the flower. Tuborgini at 2 feet is an erect primrose yellow.

Liatris is a showy and somewhat unusual perennial that has a unique feature in the way in which the flowers open first from the top of the close-packed spike. They are slightly fluffy in appearance. *L. callilepsis* is bright carmine, and flowers during the months of July to September.

Lobelia fulgens, a particularly effective plant with crimson leaves and stems, has scarlet flowers growing in spikes and the colour combination of foliage and flowers is superb. It needs plenty of water and although it will winter in the ground in mild regions, in colder districts it is better lifted in late autumn and replanted in the late spring. Whether they winter inside or out, they will usually need dividing up in the spring, for they increase nicely.

Lupins are excellent for brightening up gardens, especially in late summer. The Russell types (*Lupinus polyphyllus*) are all sturdy, with spikes of bright flowers. They appear to succeed in all types of soil, except those over rich or very chalky. There are many named varieties to choose from, such as Apple Blossom (soft pink), Canary Bird (yellow), Cynthia Knight (violet and white), Heatherglow (wine-purple), Nellie B. Allen (salmon-orange), Thundercloud (dark violet and blue) and York Minster (pale rose and cream).

Paeonies take time to establish and, once established, should be left in peace. These are not for the impatient gardener, but are so very lovely when in flower, that one feels completely rewarded by the result. They all flower in June, grow 2 to 3 feet in height and are scented, with a slender growth, and large, deeply serrated leaves. These leaves turn to reddish-bronze in the autumn. Two particularly lovely varieties are Mme Emilie Lemoine, ivory white, and Reine Hortense, pale lilac-salmon. Both produce a double form of flower.

Papaver (Oriental Poppies) are perennial poppies that are easily grown from seed, look delightful in the garden, and are excellent for cutting for the house. The flowers last longer if cut just as the buds have burst, but should have their stem ends seared in a flame for 30 seconds before placing in water, to prolong their life. There is a seed collection of 'art shades' obtainable that gives most unusual forms of colour in their range. Papavers can remain in the ground indefinitely, and if dead-headed, will probably give a second blooming later in the year. The seed heads are often used in flower decorations.

Penstemon is a very useful plant bearing tall, graceful spikes of tubular flowers, most of them perennials. It is possible to get mixed seeds in a choice variety of colours which can be grown as hardy annuals, but, if named varieties are wanted,

Lunaria (*left*) and Nigella

it is wiser to choose perennials, and then the numbers in the garden can be added to each year. They should not be cut down before the frosts are over. *P. barbatus* (syn. *Chelone barbata*) is bright scarlet and very striking, while *P. confertus* (syn. *Procerus*) varies from creamy-white to a sulphur-yellow. Heights of the Penstemon vary from 1 to 3 feet and the colours vary through white, pink and blue, to purple.

Phlomis, the Jerusalem Sage, is a low, shrubby plant with silver foliage and spikes of large yellow or mauve flowers. It is a plant suited to a hot, dry position.

Phlox flower from July to September. They are hardy and easy to grow, but allergic to hot, dry wind and excessive rain and are obtainable in plenty of gay colours, which brighten up the border, and require little or no support. A vast number of named varieties are available, but there is an attractive new white variety with a greenish eye, called Snowball, and another, *P. Norah leigh,* with variegated foliage of green and primrose. The flower is purple, but as is the case of most foliage plants this is unimportant.

Phygelius capensis (Cape Fuchsia) a half-hardy shrub with tubular orange-scarlet flowers and bronze leaves, likes a warm sunny corner, where it makes a decorative and extremely vivid patch of colour.

Papaver orientalis

Phytolacca is an unusual but attractive plant, popular with flower arrangers, which has rose-pink flowers followed by green fruit. These pass through green then red, to reach their final colour which is that of a ripe blackberry, growing in a corn-cob shape. They grow best in a warm position with good drainage, and associate well with white or very pale flowers. **Pimpinella major rosea** may be considered a rather humble

Romneya coulteri, the Californian Tree Poppy

subject to be included in this list, for it is a hardy annual herb. It comes from the wild variety *P. anisum*, which comes from Greece and can be sown in well-drained soil in a warm position where it is to remain. It grows to 2 feet, looking like pink cow parsley, and like the cow parsley of the hedgerows it has the same ethereal appearance. Against a grey stone wall, in association with slightly more solid blue flowers, and grey-foliaged plants, one would certainly not suspect its rather plebian origin.

Potentilla likes a sunny spot and is excellent as a front of the border plant. They are mostly single flowered with strawberry-type leaves and quite hardy. William Rollinson is semi-double flowered, dark orange with yellow centres and flowers from July to September.

Pulmonaria (Lungwort) is a very distinctive plant, which is ideal for the front of a border.

Romneya coulteri (Californian Tree Poppy) is a grey foliaged perennial, with deeply serrated small leaves growing up tall stems and carrying the most lovely white, poppy-like flowers with satiny petals and golden stamens. It sometimes takes a little time to settle, but once at home, and cut down to the ground in late autumn, it will reappear each summer with increasing growth. It likes full sun and seems grateful for the shelter of a wall. It does not require staking. The large flowers follow each other in quick succession and it is also useful as it blooms on well into the autumn.

Potentilla

Rosemary Rose is a wonderful rose to plant among mixed flowers and this particular floribunda associates so well with very many of the summer flowers that have already been listed, that it really must have a place among them. It has steely-purple leaves that keep their colour, and so are an asset even without the roses which are deep pink, small, flat and compact, with a rich fragrance. It flowers again in September and is very useful at that time of the year.

Salpiglossis sinuata is one of the most unusual half-hardy annuals that is very easily grown, and yet so seldom seen. About 2 feet tall, with trumpet-shaped flowers it has some of the most unusual colours and can be found, veined with gold, containing among them purples, mauves, oranges, yellows, mahogany and reds.

Thalictrum aquilegifolium has very attractive foliage that resembles that of *Aquilegia*. The fluffy heads of the dainty

The shrubby Veronicas (*Hebe*)
are easily propogated either
from cuttings or from seed.

Rosa vividflora and Briar Rose (*right*)

flowers appear in pinkish-mauve. About 2 feet high, it is a delightful plant, light and airy to look at providing, like the *Pimpinella major rosea,* a good contrast against heavier plants.

Verbascum (Mullein) are rather stately plants that have tall flower spikes covered with small flowers. Some have pale grey woolly foliage and woolly stems, for instance *V.C.L. Adams*, soft yellow flowers. *V. Cotswold Gem* which has rosy-amber flowers, and *V. Pink Domino* with deep rose flowers do not have woolly foliage, but rather leathery looking dark green leaves and stems. All grow to a height of $3\frac{1}{2}$ to $4\frac{1}{2}$ feet and can be grown as biennials, flowering from June to August.

Veronica (Hebes) can be obtained in many varieties from which a selection for the garden can be made, most of them hardy perennials. Two varieties are specially recommended for the summer months – *V. gentianoides variegata*, which has variegated yellow and green foliage, with small spikes of pale blue flowers, and the new *V. teacrium* 'Blue Fountain' that has deep rich blue flowers.

Zauschneria californica, the Californian Fuchsia, is late flowering and ideal for the front of a border. It has greyish leaves and tubular, scarlet flowers. It needs a dry, sunny area.

THE GARDEN IN AUTUMN

Autumn tasks

By the beginning of September the autumn flowers are displaying their rich colours, the foliage of trees, shrubs, and plants is deepening, berries are ripening and the evenings are beginning to shorten. There is a certain crispness in the air and one should realize that all too soon the first frosts will arrive. This means that the autumn tasks must soon be finished. The garden is still full of colour at this time of the year so that it is quite difficult to look a year ahead, to decide whether there are any changes to be made in the general lay-out of the garden, and whether there are any different plants that must be added for the following year.

Chrysanthemum

Aster

Autumn is a busy time, for many things must be planted for the following spring and summer and bulbs, perennials and the young biennials must all be bedded down for the winter. The first job at this time can be a pleasant stroll, with notebook and pencil, to check the plants that are at present flowering, in case some of the less well-known beauties of autumn are not present.

Probably the most popular autumn-flowering plants are the Chrysanthemums. This genus comprises more than a hundred species of annual and perennial plants and it is possible to select a colour to suit almost any colour arrangement or soil type. Although chrysanthemums can be made to flower at any time of the year, most people regard them as a late summer and autumn flower of the open garden. The growing period can be extended by late varieties that flower under glass.

The perennial border plant that is usually known as the Michaelmas Daisy comprises numerous varieties of *Aster novi-belgii* and together with Dahlias, Solidago (Golden Rod) and Zinnias is frequently seen in the autumn garden. Lovely as these old favourites are, however, there are many other subjects and newer varieties of the established favourites that should also be considered.

Dwarf variety of *Kniphofia*

Newer varieties

Acidanthera, which blooms in September to October, has triangular white flowers, with blackish-maroon centres and a very sweet scent. These grow up the stalks in a manner similar to that of a rather delicate gladiolus. The corms should be planted in April, May or June of the same year in which they are to bloom. Sometimes they will disappear during the winter, never to be seen again, but the corms are not at all expensive and some more can easily be planted for the following year. They look so delightful in the garden and it is unusual to have flowers of this type so late in the year. *A. murielae* is the only species of this most delightful plant usually cultivated in Britain.

Anaphalis yedoensis is an attractive addition to the garden during the late autumn. It is a tall plant (3 feet) with narrow grey-green leaves that grow all the way up the stems, at the top of which are bunched the small everlasting silver-white flowers.

Anemone japonica is a very welcome pale pink, or white, hardy perennial that reaches $1\frac{1}{2}$ to 2 feet in height and flowers during the autumn. These flowers are single in form and they possess extremely decorative stamens. Several flowers grow on each stem.

Gentiana sind-ornata

Prickly poppy (*left*) and
Anemone hupensis

Argemone mexicana (Devil's Fig or Prickly Poppy) is a new hardy annual which has a long flowering period and prefers a sunny position and light soils. It comes into flower before September but remains in flower during that month and is probably appreciated even more then, than it is earlier on. The flowers are delicate primrose-coloured and it has a soft grey-green foliage. The seed pods are distinctive and decorative.

A. grandiflora has grey-white, prickly leaves and creamy flowers from July to September.

Amaryllis belladonna is often known as the Belladonna Lily and has umbels of large fragrant flowers that are pale pink on the outside shading to white at the centre. It is a very beautiful, nearly hardy bulbous plant that should be planted against a warm south wall. The leaves come first during the late winter or early spring and die down in summer while the flowerstalks are thrown up to bloom from September to October.

Once established, this plant should be left undisturbed. The variety 'Hathor' is excellent. It is a lovely white. Another good one is 'Parkeri', a deep pink, $1\frac{1}{2}$ to 2 feet high.

Colchicum, better known as the Autumn Crocus, are autumn-flowering bulbs, which have the unusual characteristic of thrusting up their flowers straight from the ground before any foliage appears. They start flowering from October onwards, producing broad leafy foliage in the spring. The flowers are generally pink or rose-lilac in colour, although there is a pure white form obtainable. It is often known as the Meadow Saffron.

Fuchsia has an unusual variety, Cape Fuchsia, that is described as being half-hardy, but is generally quite robust in all but the very coldest positions. It has tubular, deep orange flowers with plum-brown foliage and grows to a height of 2 to 4 feet.

Fuchsia 'Mrs Popple' is a hardy fuchsia that is very colourful with purple and magenta flowers and *F.* 'Madame Cornelius' has red and white flowers. Both these last named Fuchsias continue blooming until November and are 2 feet high. There is also a dwarf variety called Tom Thumb suitable for the

Nerine bowdenii is easy to grow and can be left for most of the year. (*right*) the Autumn Crocus, *Colchicum*

rockery that bears large red and pink flowers and also flowers until November. All fuchsias should be cut down at Christmas to ground level and then covered lightly with bracken or ashes, and left to shoot again in the spring.

Gentiana sind-ornata likes autumn sun whenever possible, and this low-growing perennial with lovely rich blue trumpet flowers deserves the position of its choice. It grows 4 to 6 inches high and is attractive in a sink garden. The *Gentiana sino-ornata* does not like lime, and prefers a fairly moist soil with some peat, and if suitably sited, will spread into a wonderful blue carpet in October.

Kniphofia is usually known as the Red Hot Poker and has a variety called 'Macowani' that flowers in October, later than the other types, and has slender orange-red 2 foot high spikes. *K. snowdoni* also continues to show its coral spikes in October. This is an excellent genus for use in 'island beds' of various herbaceous plants set in a lawn.

Rhus cotinus, the Smoke Tree (*left*) has very attractive autumn foliage, as does the Stag's-horn Sumach (*Rhus typhina*).

Liatris has a white variety that flowers later than the lilac one that has already been mentioned among summer flowers. It should be planted in a light soil in a dry situation and the seed should be started under a cloche or in a greenhouse in spring.

Monarda (Bergamot) gives a pleasant fragrance and is somewhat unusual, since it has square stems with brightly coloured bracts forming part of the flower-head. *M. didyma*, with pink, red, or scarlet flowers and hairy leaves, starts to flower in July, but continues until the end of September and is 2 to 3 feet high.

Montbretia laxifolia has narrow, straight leaves up to 12 inches long, with cream and pinkish-orange flowers on loose spikes, from September to October. It is not reliably hardy on cold soils and it is safer to lift and store like gladioli in October.

Nerine bowdeni (Guernsey Lily) produces large umbels of pink flowers in late September and October. It is hardy in southern regions but likes to grow at the foot of a south wall if

Montbretia laxifolia flowers during the months of September and October, while *Anaphalis yedoensis* is an attractive addition to the late autumn garden (*right*)

it is at all possible, or a similar sheltered situation.

Polygonum baldshuanicum, the Russian Vine, is a fast growing climber which flowers in the autumn. Its exceptionally quick growth makes it ideal for covering dull walls.

Rhus cotinus (Smoke Tree) has the most beautiful soft foliage of yellow and red in autumn. Although it grows to a height of 15 feet eventually, this is over a considerable period of time. This shrub does best in a dry position.

Salvia patens is a wonderful half-hardy perennial, which has large, free-blooming flowers sky-blue in colour. It will winter outside if it is given a little protection but it is sometimes advisable to lift the tubers in late October and store them in sand. They can be started into growth under glass in early April.

Schizostylis (Kaffir Lily) flowers in October until December, resembling small dainty Gladioli and is obtainable in both pink and red. 'Mrs Hegarty', a satiny rose-pink, always seems to give good results, and usually has a slightly longer flowering period than many of the other varieties.

Bergamot (*Monarda*) are leafy hardy herbaceous perennials that have a very aromatic foliage and flower during July and August.

125

Galtonia has white bell-shaped flowers along stems that reach about a foot in height.

Sedum spectabile (Autumn Glory) gives good heads of pinkish flowers all the summer, but in autumn the flower-heads slowly turn to red, then dry on the plant to dark brown. They can be cut and used dry in winter flower arrangements. *S. maximum atropurpureum* is a slightly taller Sedum and has purple-brown fleshy leaves and stems. The flowers, too, have similar coloured flat heads composed of a number of very tiny flowers. They last a long time on the plant and make a good colour contrast with the brighter flowers of autumn. *S. cauticola* has rosy-purple flowers and glaucous grey-green leaves during the early autumn. It is rather different from the other varieties of this plant as it is a trailing form, but is very attractive. *S. cauticola* will die down in the winter. Probably the most striking of all the Sedums is *S. spathulifolium*. This variety *purpureum* flowers in May and June but in the autumn the large white leaves turn to a spectacular scarlet.

Tricyrtis (Toad Lily) are not spectacular, but they are un- usual Japanese plants, with oval, pointed leaves growing up the stems and curiously shaped flowers similar to a lily at the top. These are mauve-striped, and they like a shady position although they should be given a position near a path where they can be seen preferably in a light soil containing peat. They flower late, which is just as well, for they can very easily be overshadowed by more pushing neighbours.

In September or October the biennials that were sown in June and then transferred to nursery beds, can be planted into their flowering positions for the following year. Among these are Aquilegias, Canterbury Bells, Wallflowers, Sweet Williams, Foxgloves, Delphiniums, Lupins, Oriental Poppies, Forget-me-nots and Verbaseum.

The spring and summer-flowering bulbs and rhizomes should be planted in October, such as Allium, Anemones, Hardy Cyclamen, Fritillary, Galanthus, Galtonia, Iris (English), Dutch, and Spanish) and Lilium (Hardy species). Tulips species and Nerines should be planted in November.

Belladonna Lily. *Amaryllis belladonna*

Salvia patens is a half-hardy perennial with large sky-blue flowers.

FLOWER ARRANGEMENT

Some of the plants mentioned for flower arrangement have also been referred to elsewhere in this book, but so often a plant that is grown, and admired for its beauty in the garden, does not necessarily strike one as a subject for flower arrangement. This applies particularly to the foliage. So often only the flowers are considered for flower arrangement and at first it is not realized that perhaps just one leaf can create, in an arrangement of other material, the vital ingredient to give that arrangement individuality and personality, the 'difference' that turns flower arranging into an art. Anyone with sufficient money can buy costly flowers from a florist, and put them into an expensive vase to produce a pleasing result, but there is no art in this, just money. The true flower arranger is one with a 'seeing' eye, who can put together three twigs, five leaves, and one flower to make a truly lovely picture in an empty sardine tin. The following list is aimed at accustoming the reader to using this 'seeing' eye.

Hosta leaves are invaluable, especially the variegated ones, such as *fortunei clba-picta, aurea variegata,* and *albomarginata. Bergenia* leaves are really more helpful to the flower arranger than their flower clusters, charming as they are in the spring, with their brownish fleshy stems bearing clusters of small pink flowers. The leaves, which should be immersed in a bowl of water for several hours after picking and before arranging so that they will last longer, are useful for decorations throughout the year. In the summer, when their large leaves are a wonderful solid green, they will give a helpful solidity at the back, or base, of summer flowers that are inclined to be 'leggy'. In autumn, the green turns to yellows, browns and flame colourings that are just right for the autumnal flowers. In winter their colouring is a rich red and they can be used with the dried tassels of the red *Amaranthus candatus* and dried *Sedum spectabile* 'Autumn Glory' heads, which turn to a brownish red and blend extremely well with the other 'ingredients'.

Large-leaved plants are especially useful in simple, uncluttered types of arrangements. Very often, they can be set as a background to small flowers.

Rhus (Stag's-horn Sumach)

Bells of Ireland

Rosemary Rose

129

Helleborus corsicus is of immense value, flowering as it does through the worst months of winter, giving wonderful, very pale green, waxy flowers.

Alchemilla mollis is another must for the flower arranger. This feathery-flowered summer plant is an ideal companion for almost any other colour and its lime green lightness seems to look perfect with so many other flowers.

Molucella laevis (Bells of Ireland) are useful, both green and dried. Not always easily germinated, it is unusual in appearance. The flowers that grow up the stalks are very tiny and insignificant and it is the apple-green waxy circular calyx surrounding them that provides the interest. If the tiny white flowers and the uninteresting foliage are removed, either the stems and calyx can be used green, or dried, when they will become a pale biscuit shade and prove endlessly useful in autumn and winter arrangements.

Paeonies (*bottom*) have a varied colour range and are relatively easy to grow. Foxgloves, *Digitalis*, are useful for flower arrangements.

Nerine bowdenii is easy to grow under a south wall where it can be left all the year round. The foliage, strap-like and a dark shiny green, comes first, then dies back and the flowers appear. These bulbuous subjects look more like a delicate greenhouse plant and to find them growing outside in late September appears a miracle. The flowers are similar to a small lily with deeply cut petals of cerise pink with long stamens.

Schizostylis (Kaffir Lily) flowers and foliage resemble very small gladioli and appear in the garden between October and December when the pink, sometimes red, flowers are so very useful. They have creeping rhizomes, not bulbs, that like to be planted in a sheltered position, and are very easily grown. The variety named Mrs Hegarty is a satiny rose-pink and seems to be the popular one. Although there is a red variety the nurseries do not seem to list it and pink is such an unusual shade in the late autumn. They last well in water.

Digitalis (Foxgloves) are obtainable in unusual colours, and because of their 'points' are extremely useful to the flower arranger, especially in large arrangements. They combine well with the roundness of double paeonies and luckily both are out at the same time.

Nicotiana 'Lime Green' (*left*) is very suitable for all green arrangements while *Zinnia* can be found in most sizes and colours.

Cardoon leaves seem to grow in all sizes, and their soft grey blends with everything. There are always a few leaves to be found even in winter, but when cut the stems *must* be put in boiling water for a depth of about an inch for a period of 30 seconds, and then stood in a bucketful of cold water for several hours to prevent them from wilting. It is wise to treat all cut foliage in this way, except some of the smaller leaves, like *Hosta* and *Arum italicum*, and all the ferns, which must be immersed in a bowl or bath of cold water for several hours before using. Woolly foliage such as *Stachys lanata* (Lambs Ears) should not be immersed because it would destroy the bloom.

There are two roses which should be mentioned here, both very useful for arrangements. The first is the Rosemary Rose, because its purple-pewter foliage is invaluable for colour and the other is the old-fashioned green rose – *R. viridiflora*. Some people are rather rude about the latter variety but it is certainly unusual and quite unlike other roses. The flowers and buds are small, growing in clusters and they have a long flowering period. When the flowers are fully open the petals show that they are streaked lightly with reddish-brown, which suggests

Decorative grasses (*also far right*)

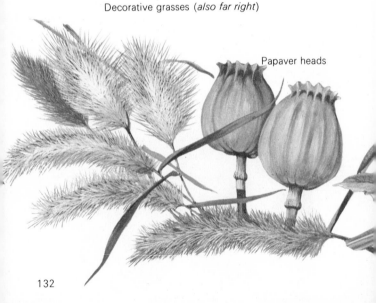

Papaver heads

that this touch of colour could be emphasized with foliage, and perhaps other flowers, of the same reddish-brown.

Lunaria (Honesty) is grown mostly for its silvery white seed pods that can be dried for winter decorations. Although the pods are quite useful when they are mixed with other dried material for this purpose, they are equally attractive when they are fresh. The flowers are a vivid purple at the end of May, combining well with a number of other spring flowers. Directly the flowers drop, the seed pods formed from them turn lovely deep purple. Both shape and colour of the seed pods at this stage are much more decorative than when they have been dried.

Bocconia Coral Plume is a 'must' for the flower arranger. This is rather a large plant growing sometimes to 6 feet, with sycamore-type leaves that are bronze-green above and silver-grey underneath, and with tall grey stems carrying minor stems of tiny orange-brown flowers which give it a soft, cloudy, plume-like effect even when the flowers are over.

Cardoon leaves

133

Rhus typhina laciniata (Stags Horn Sumach) is a hardy tree with very beautiful coloured foliage during the autumn and crimson plush fruits that stand up like candles. The leaves drop fairly soon after colouring but for a brief time are quite lovely combined with berries, and other autumn foliage or flowers.

Angelica archangelica usually appears on cakes, after its large tubular stems have been cut and crystallized, but it is also very useful and handsome to use fresh for arrangement. It has large green seed heads and bold foliage that turns to pale yellow in its second summer.

Iris pseudacorus variegatus is described as a Water Iris or the Yellow Flag Iris, but will grow quite well in damp garden soil. The sword-like variegated leaves are extremely useful and their variegation makes them much more interesting to give height to an all-foliage arrangement. There is also a white-flowered variety.

Zinnia are to be found in all sizes, from giants down to dwarfs, and in all colours and shades. The chrysanthemum and dahlia-flowered varities have huge blooms, many up

Xeranthemum annuum

Artemesia

to 6 inches across. The lime-green Zinnia, Envy, is comparatively new, and ideal for all-green arrangements which can include the green *Nicotiana* 'Lime Green', which is charming although it does not seem to have the scent of the white and coloured Tobacco plants, and *Alchemilla mollis*.

Honesty

Helichrysum bracieatum

Limonium sinuatum

Sedum maximum atropurpureum is another member of the useful Sedum family, but taller than most of the varieties ($1\frac{1}{2}$ feet). It is very uncommon and very beautiful, with fleshy leaves of mahogany-purple climbing up the stem, and flat broad heads of similar coloured flowers from August to October *Achillea* 'Gold Plate' is the best variety for drying because it keeps its yellow colour well and blends with the other dried flowers and seed heads that help to make our winter flower arrangements. *Atriplex* with its red foliage in summer, which is so useful, also has quite interesting seed heads which dry well for winter.

These are just a few of the plants with which to practise the 'seeing eye' but there are many more, including vegetables and fruit, that look unusual and gay when arranged as a 'still life' in the early autumn. There are, of course, no hard or fast rules for the methods of flower arrangement but practice with a small amount of the foliage and flowers that are plentiful in the garden will soon enable the art to be developed.

WEEDS AND THEIR TREATMENT

Garden weeds differ in treatment according to their type and these will be listed under their separate headings.

Annual weeds such as Charlock, Knotgrass, Groundsel, Pimpernel, and Chickweed are the easiest to get rid of, providing they are not allowed to seed. In the young stages they can be hoed, otherwise they must be handpulled. As they are shallow rooted they can be turned over when digging.

Creeping weeds are Trefoil, Nettle, Celandine, Dead Nettle, Ground Elder, Bindweed and these perennial weeds have underground stems or spreading roots that help them to grow very quickly, so when such weeds appear in the garden immediate action should be taken. Every portion of root should be grubbed up and burnt at once, because, if any of these weeds are neglected, they will quickly over-run the garden.

Annual weeds (*from left to right*);
Chickweed, Groundsel, Fat Hen

In addition to grubbing out at once, particular care must be taken whenever digging, and especially in spring and autumn, to remove every piece of weed root seen, for each tiny particle left in, or on, the soil is able to grow and form a new plant.

Deep rooted Perennial weeds such as Thistle, Mares Tail, Couch Grass, Dock and Bracken can only be eradicated by deep digging, making certain that no portion of any root is left in the soil. All these roots must also be burned.

Lawn weeds, almost all of which are perennial, are Plantain, Yarrow, Clover, Dandelion and Daisy. To kill Plantain and Dandelion roots, the crown of the weed can be pierced deeply, which will kill its growth. Yarrow should be grubbed out. Clover and Daisies should also be grubbed out and lawn sand applied. This can be obtained from most seedsmen and it will destroy weeds and feed the fine grasses.

Creeping weeds (*from left to right*);
Ground Elder, Bindweed, Trefoil

Perennial weeds (*from left to right*):
Thistle, Mare's Tail, Dock

There are more and more chemical aids to weed killing coming on to the market all the time, and no-one would wish to turn down any available help with this tedious and unattractive task. One preparation containing Paraquat is useful because it is a kind of chemical hoe destroying the green tops of anything it touches, but not contaminating the soil. This means that it can be used on rose beds, shrubberies, or anywhere else where garden plants are growing high enough to make it possible to avoid wetting their foliage when applying the liquid to the weed. A watering can should be used, fitted with a dribble bar, which is obtainable where you buy the Paraquat, and enables the liquid to be applied more accurately to the lawn.

Simazene weed killers are also useful, particularly for paths and drives, and it will keep them clear of weeds for a year or more. It is non-soluble and therefore will not spread into neighbouring lawns or beds. The chemical forms a film over

Lawn weeds (*from left to right*):
Ribwort Plantain, Clover,
Dandelion

the surface in which nothing will germinate for about a year if the film remains unbroken. The hoe cannot be used of course, as this would break the film and destroy its efficiency. It is better to weed before applying Simazene for it is a preventive rather than a killer and if applied to weed free surfaces it will keep them weed free. When using any type of chemical weed killer the watering can, dribble bar, rose, or any other utensil that has been used must be thoroughly washed with soapy water after use.

Whatever methods are used to control the spread of weeds it must be remembered that prevention of the spread of weeds in the initial stages is by far the best method. The smothering effect of weeds on any plants starts immediately the seeds are up, and early weeding is imperative. If large areas of weeds must be cleared it is sometimes possible to use a weed burner. This will destroy vegetation and seeds but will not reach deep roots so will not kill weeds immediately.

PLANTS TO GROW FOR SCENT

To grow plants for their scent sounds contradictory because in most people's minds the one is associated with the other. Whether or not it is due to the constant research and efforts of horticulturists to produce better and newer variations of old favourites with larger flowers in newer colour ranges, the fact remains that many plants today appear to be losing their scent, and have not the rich perfume of bygone days. Scent is evocative of many happy moments and the heady mixtures of perfumes from the garden can coat the pill of some of the more boring jobs that have to be undertaken in that garden, and all gardens, of course.

Summer naturally brings a greater variety of scented plants starting with the humble Night-scented Stock, a Cinderella among hardy annuals that is small and nothing special to look at, yet in the quiet summer evenings it fills the air with a perfume that belies both its size and appearance.

Mignonette too, although more attractive than the Night-scented Stock, and sometimes to be seen as a front-of-the-border plant, is another surprise for those that confuse appearance with scent. Wallflowers, growing under an open

Dianthus gratianopolitanus,
Border Pinks (*centre*) and
Dianthus allwoodii (*right*)

window in late spring can be replaced later by white Nicotiana. The coloured Tobacco plants have not, for some reason, the same heady scent. White summer-flowering Jasmine, the best scented being *Jasmine officinale*, is one of the oldest 'common' types, but so many of the newer varieties, although more elegant in some ways, have sacrificed much of their scent for the 'new look'. Of the correctly named *Syringa vulgaris* (Lilac) probably the best to choose are Madame Lemoine and Charles Joly, both well scented varieties.

Nicotiana and Mignonette, both have a perfume that belies their appearance.

Lavender spica, a blue lavender, is a good variety and although there are both white and pink lavenders available, they do not seem to be such robust growers, and do not conform with memories of lavender, which was always blue. *Monarda didyma* (Bergamot) is not only a favourite border plant, but the entire plant, flowers, leaves and roots, is strongly aromatic. Cambridge Scarlet is a good red, and Croftway Pink, with pink flowers, equally good. *Camomile,* the low growing variety, is an excellent herb for growing between the stones in a path, for when walked upon it emits a sweet scent, as do the Thymes. There are many different Thymes, but the prostrate ones will suit the purpose best of course. Cowslips can be grown easily from seed and Violets can be grown rather grandly in greenhouse or frame, but their perfume is then unable to mix with that of the rest of the garden. *V. odorata* has the true scent and can be grown outside, in little sheltered pockets in the rock garden, or by the edge of paths. On a wet day the leaves smell strongly, even if the plant is not in flower. Lilies, both Lily-of-the-Valley and the hardy border types, Sweet Williams, which belong to the Carnation family and Dianthus have lost much of their scent nowadays. *D. caesius* still has the original clove perfume, however, and the old cottage pinks and the Border Carnations are all richly scented. Others for the list are Rosemary, Sweet Rocket, Hyacinth, ten-week Stock and the 'old-fashioned' shrub Roses, such as the Provence rose (Cabbage Rose), Damask, Moss, and Gallica roses, and the Briar Rose (*Rosa rubiginosa*). The flowers of the Briar rose do not smell, but the stems and leaves do. It is an untidy plant, but grown as a hedge, and clipped fairly often, it can be kept neat enough, and on summer evenings especially after a shower, when the air is damp and warm, the garden is filled with its perfume.

In winter, sweet scent is given by the Viburnums, especially *V. fragrans,* the winter flowering Honeysuckles, and by *Hamamelis mollis, Chimonanthus praecox fragrans, Daphne mezereum, D. laureola* and *D. odora,* but in this quiet time of the year, the perfume, too, is quiet, stealing out mostly towards the end of the day, as if to remind one that the richness of the summer air will be back. Scent is especially important during winter, when it is fully appreciated.

Honeysuckle

Lavandula

Lily of the Valley

143

DECORATIVE TREES

Decorative trees, delightful as they are, need a little thought before planting. Although most trees are comparatively slow growers it is as well to remember that something which appears to be no larger than a shrub for the first few years will eventually reach a height of from 12 to 50 feet with, in most cases, width in proportion, giving shade where there was no shade, altering the sky line, perhaps even blotting out a view.

The trees mentioned here do not grow very tall, and should be suitable for most gardens of medium size, but their position *will* require thought.

Acer palmatum dissectum atropurpureum (Maple) is a decorative small tree with finely cut purple-red leaves in summer that turn to fiery red in autumn. It slowly attains a height of 12 feet but is useful for its colourful splendour.

Aesculus (Horse Chestnut) has the 'Red Horse Chestnut' *A. carnea* that eventually grows into a tall tree and is such a slow grower that it can be planted with safety in the average size garden. Its deep pink flowers and attractive leaves will make

Fruit of the flowering Crab (*left*) and flowers of *Cercis siliquastrum*

Acer palmatum atropurpureum

Prunus amanogawa

a feature on lawn or boundary.

Arbutus unedo (The Strawberry Tree) is a beautiful evergreen tree with dark green leaves and pendant lily-of-the-valley type flowers, followed by orange strawberry-like fruit in October-November.

Betula verrucosa (Silver Birch) is one of our most charming and decorative small trees. The lightness of the branch system, the grace of the small catkins and delicate little leaves and the silvery bark, make it an ideal tree to have as a companion for the spring bulbs. In winter the bark gleams in the winter sunshine.

Catalpa bignonioides (Indian Bean Tree) has large ornamental leaves, and flowers growing in erect spikes, that are yellow and purple-spotted white and replaced in winter by long bean shaped fruits. It likes a sheltered, sunny position, flowers in July and grows to a height of 25 feet.

Cercis siliquastrum (Judas Tree) is a small tree bearing rosy-lilac flowers resembling a pink laburnum before the leaves in May and June, with attractive seed pods during the winter. The flowers are borne on the stems and trunk.

Eucalyptus gunnii is one of the hardiest of the Eucalyptus species, and grows fairly quickly into a handsome evergreen tree, with aromatic leaves and wood. The young foliage is silver-blue. *E. perriniana* is another variety that is also quick-growing and has grey circular leaves and silvery stems. This can be pruned hard in April to encourage young growth, or allowed to develop into a tall tree. It is not fully hardy in all parts of Great Britain.

Laburnum vossii is a bright and cheerful May-flowering tree with long racemes of yellow flowers. *L. v. autumnale* bears flowers periodically all through the summer and early autumn.

Magnolia soulangeana is one of the hardiest, and easiest to grow, of the Magnolias. The large white tulip-shaped flowers are flushed with purple on the outside of the petals. It is a deciduous tree, flowering in April-May and reaches a height of 20 feet. *M. stellata* is compact, twiggy, growing to a height of 6 to 7 feet and almost more bush than tree, but the white semi-double, fragrant flowers that come before the leaves in

Philadelphus or Mock Orange

March and April are very lovely and smaller and more graceful than those of *M. soulangeana*, although easily damaged by wind.

Malus (Pyrus) are flowering Crabs that give a wonderful display of flower in April-May, followed in autumn by very ornamental fruit and foliage. *M. Coronaria charlottae* has large semi-double, scented, shell-pink flowers in spring and richly coloured foliage in the autumn. *M. eley*, purple foliage with wine red flowers in May and reddish purple cherry-like fruit in early autumn.

Prunus (Flowering Cherry) has a variety *P. amanogawa* that is an ideal flowering Cherry for a small space in a garden or courtyard because it grows straight upwards like a Lombardy Poplar, with almond-scented flowers of palest pink. *P. grandiflora* (Yukon) is an unusual Cherry. With large, semi-double, greenish-yellow flowers and a brownish tinge in its foliage it has a completely different colouring from most of the other spring flowering trees, that usually have white or pink flowers.

Lilac

Magnolia soulangeana

PRESERVATION OF FLOWERS AND FOLIAGE

Glycerine

There are several ways of preserving flowers, leaves and seed-heads from the garden for use in the house in the winter. The small effort required to do this will give excellent rewards in the form of arrangements that will last the whole of the winter. It is quite a good idea to re-arrange the dried and preserved material in different ways and in different containers from time to time to give it a changed look. Not more than one dried arrangement should be made for each room, and one small vase for fresh flowers should be kept. Although the garden will yield most of the material needed for preservation there are one or two things from the hedgerows and woods that can be easily preserved, and which will give you added scope for your arrangements.

The first and almost the easiest method of preserving leaves and sprays of leaves is known as the glycerine method. A solution of one part glycerine to two parts warm water (warm water mixes more easily than cold with the glycerine) should be made and put in a wide necked jar, or bucket, allowing a

The Red Horse Chestnut,
Aeculus carnea

depth of four inches in which to stand the stems of the branches to be preserved. It is as well to have the glycerine-and-water mixture ready by the end of July, because any sprays of foliage must be picked when the sap is still rising so that they can drink up the mixture. If left until the sap starts to run back into the roots, the absorption of the mixture, and therefore the preservation, will not be so successful. This applies particularly to hard-stemmed trees and shrubs such as beech, laurel, skimmia, sweet chestnut, evergreen magnolia, and rhododendron sprays, all of which are suitable for this treatment. It is a help if the ends of these hard-stemmed subjects are split for about an inch to allow easier absorption while standing in the mixture.

It is interesting to experiment with untried plant material and if necessary to make another mixture, using similar proportions of glycerine to water, to start another collection of foliage because it is better to give all the foliage plenty of room and thus absorb the mixture properly.

Preserving foliage in glycerine.

About three weeks is usually long enough for the glycerine and water to become sufficiently absorbed, but this can be checked at intervals. When the surface of the leaves starts to become oily it shows that they cannot drink any more and are ready to be taken out and laid on sheets of newspaper until they are required for use. They should *not* be put into water at any time, once they are preserved, and this applies to all preserved and dried material. Sprays of blackberry and wild roses will glycerine well, if the sprays are mature, and have not flowered, when picked. Small leaves, such as Lily-of-the-Valley and Ivy should be immersed in the liquid. These latter can also be pressed, but will be a paler brown, and brittle.

Pressing and drying

The pressing method of preservation can be used for ferns, chestnut leaves, raspberry, and bergenia leaves, ivy, bracken and large autumn leaves. These should be laid flat between newspaper taking care to keep all the leaves and fronds separate from each other and weighting them down so that an even pressure is maintained until they are thoroughly dried.

If there are any specially colourful autumn leaves to be dried they can be placed between sheets of newspaper and pressed with a cool iron. *Hosta* leaves, which turn golden brown in autumn, can also be ironed. Because leaves dry more quickly under the iron, colour is better preserved.

Flowers selected for drying for winter use should be cut just before the flowers reach maturity. They must be tied up in small bunches and left hanging upside-down in a dry, dark cupboard or attic where there is good air circulation.

The darkness will prevent the colours from fading and they should be left hanging in the dark until they are required for use in the house. Flowers that can be treated in this manner are Delphiniums, Larkspur, Love-lies-Bleeding, Sedums, Hop flowers, Bolota and Astilbes. All foliage should be removed before drying, and the flowers displayed with ferns or evergreens when they are required.

Grasses, especially variegated types, are very useful for graceful and artistic floral displays. They can often be used to great effect with Pampas Grass flower heads, where the great fluffy heads are enhanced by the thin, willowy pieces of grass.

Borax and preserving seed heads

Another method of drying flowers is by using powdered Borax, which will keep the shape of the flowers as well as their colours. The bottom of a fairly deep box should be covered with a good layer of Borax, all leaves must be stripped from the flowers and the stems shortened. Then they must be stood upright on the Borax and more Borax carefully put around each flower, the petals smoothed down as they are covered to keep their shape. A sheet of paper must be put on top of the buried flowers and they must be left for about three weeks. When the dried flowers are removed from the powder, the petals will be very brittle. Most open-faced flowers can be preserved in this way, but the flowers must be free from moisture before they are buried. Longer stemmed flowers should be laid face down in a long box on a layer of Borax, then the box filled as before, with the stems sticking out.

Large, flat leaves and flowers are best preserved by pressing.

Some flowers, such as Hydrangea, Molucella, and Acanthus, dry better if, after removing all the leaves, the stem ends are placed in about an inch of warm water. When the water has been absorbed the flowers will be dry. Somehow these flowers seem to dry better by this contradiction-in-terms method, and a warm kitchen is just the place for drying both these, and seed heads. The best way of drying Achilleas too, is by placing the stems in shallow water, and in this case, sprinkling the flower heads with a little Borax while they are drying, which will ensure they retain their colour.

When seed-heads are preserved they should be as ripe as possible when picked. After picking, the leaves should be removed and they should then be hung upside down in a warm place to finish drying. Suitable seed-heads that can be selected for drying are Atriplex, Foxgloves, Lupins, Poppy, Iris, Angelica, Dock, Cardoon and Teasel.

Use of Borax to preserve flowers and seed heads ready for drying (*right*)

CHRISTMAS DECORATIONS

As Christmas approaches some of these dried leaves and seed-heads can be transformed into Christmas arrangements quite easily by painting them with white shoe cleaner, which has the advantage of drying quickly, and being easily washed off any unintentional destination such as floors and tables.

When any painted foliage is dry, glass glitter can be used lightly to give a sparkle to tips of leaves and seed-heads, to outline the edges of small leaves and to simulate frost on branches Glass glitter can be bought in many shops and applied with the aid of a small brush and a bottle of clear gum. The material is 'painted' with the gum wherever the glitter is required and while the gum is still wet the plant should be sprinkled with glitter. Silver glitter, or glitter in many other colours, can also be bought and used in the manner described as required. A pepper pot is a good method of distribution and a newspaper should be used to catch surplus glitter, which can then go back into the pepper pot, for use at another time. Use of glitter should not be overdone.

Evergreens can make attractive winter-time displays, especially during the Christmas period.

Scarlet ribbon can be used for making bows and loops for additional colour, and scarlet candles, baubles and pine cones painted scarlet will all look gay and festive. If one wishes to gild any dried material, and cardoon seed heads look very striking gilded it is easier to buy an aerosol spray than to paint everything by hand. This should be used in a shed or garage, however, unless one wishes to decorate the house as well.

Evergreens can also have a touch of glitter and, if holly berries are scarce, artificial berries can be bought and wired on to the holly as they would normally grow. White shoe cleaner brushed on to the branches of a Christmas tree can look very effective and aerosol cans of artificial snow can also be bought.

As the old year ends, the new year's catalogues will start to arrive, new life begins to disturb the soil, and the winter flowers are appearing. Soon the spring will be here and there is much to plan, and mistakes to remedy, for the garden merry-go-round will start again very soon.

Hollywreaths are traditionally made at Christmas. The easiest method of construction is to wire the stems to a circular wire frame. Moss helps to give a pleasing background.

BOOKS TO READ

A Dictionary of the Flowering Plants and Ferns by J. C. Willis. Cambridge University Press, 1966.

Clematis by Christopher Lloyd. Country Life, London, 1965.

Complete Flower Gardening in Pictures by Richard Sudell. Odhams Press, London.

Encyclopedia of Modern Gardening by N. P. Harvey. Spring Books, 1965.

Gardening in Colour by Frances Perry. Paul Hamlyn, London, 1967.

Gardening Plants and Designs by A. G. L. Hellyer. Collingridge, London, 1964.

Greenhouse Place of Magic by Charles H. Potter. Dutton, New York, 1967.

Natural Rock Gardening by B. H. B. Symons-Jeune. Country Life, London, 1955.

Pictorial Gardening Pearson, London, 1964.

The Flower Arranger and Her Garden by Jane Derbyshire. Pearson, London, 1967.

The Fragrant Garden by H. L. V. Fletcher. Newnes, London, 1965.

The Mixed Border by Christopher Lloyd. Collingridge, London, and Transatlantic Arts Inc., Florida, 1957.

The World of Roses by Bertram Park. Harrap, London, 1966.

Water Gardening by Frances Perry. Country Life, London, 1961.

INDEX

SOME OTHER TITLES IN THIS SERIES

Arts
Antique Furniture/Architecture/Art Nouveau for Collectors/Clocks and Watches/Glass for Collectors/Jewellery/Musical Instruments/Porcelain/Pottery/Silver for Collectors/Victoriana

Domestic Animals and Pets
Budgerigars/Cats/Dog Care/Dogs/Horses and Ponies/Pet Birds/Pets for Children/Tropical Freshwater Aquaria/Tropical Marine Aquaria

Domestic Science
Flower Arranging

Gardening
Chrysanthemums/Garden Flowers/Garden Shrubs/House Plants/Plants for Small Gardens/Roses

General Information
Aircraft/Arms and Armour/Coins and Medals/Espionage/Flags/Fortune Telling/Freshwater Fishing/Guns/Military Uniforms/Motor Boats and Boating/National Costumes of the world/Orders and Decorations/Rockets and Missiles/Sailing/Sailing Ships and Sailing Craft/Sea Fishing/Trains/Veteran and Vintage Cars/Warships

History and Mythology
Age of Shakespeare/Archaeology/Discovery of: Africa/The American West/Australia/Japan/North America/South America/Great Land Battles/Great Naval Battles/Myths and Legends of: Africa/Ancient Egypt/Ancient Greece/Ancient Rome/India/The South Seas/Witchcraft and Black Magic

Natural History
The Animal Kingdom/Animals of Australia and New Zealand/Animals of Southern Asia/Bird Behaviour/Birds of Prey/Butterflies/Evolution of Life/Fishes of the world/Fossil Man/A Guide to the Seashore/Life in the Sea/Mammals of the world/Monkeys and Apes/Natural History Collecting/The Plant Kingdom/Prehistoric Animals/Seabirds/Seashells/Snakes of the world/Trees of the world/Tropical Birds/Wild Cats

Popular Science
Astronomy/Atomic Energy/Chemistry/Computers at Work/The Earth/Electricity/Electronics/Exploring the Planets/Heredity/The Human Body/Mathematics/Microscopes and Microscopic Life/Physics/Psychology/Undersea Exploration/The Weather Guide